15 Great Pet Blogs
...And Their Most Memorable Posts

Kyla Duffy and Lowrey Mumford
Published by Happy Tails Books™, LLC

Happy Tails Books™ publishes books about the responsible acquisition and care of pets. A portion of profits from each sale is donated back to animal rescue and welfare organizations.

15 Great Pet Blogs And Their Most Memorable Posts by Kyla Duffy and Lowrey Mumford

Published by Happy Tails Books™, LLC www.happytailsbooks.com

© Copyright 2011 Happy Tails Books™, LLC. Printed and bound in the United States of America. All Rights Reserved. No part of this book may be reproduced in any form or by any electronic or mechanical means, including information storage and retrieval systems, without written permission from the publisher.

The publisher gratefully acknowledges the bloggers who participated in the creation of this book and who regularly entertain and educate pet lovers about responsible pet care.

Any brand names mentioned in this book are registered trademarks and the property of their owners. The author and publishing company make no claims to them.

Photo Credits: Photographers reserve the rights to photos used in the book. Blog photos are credited in their respective chapters.

Title Page Photo: Neil Brogan and Nigel Buggers, Life With Dogs

Introduction Page Photo (cat in sink): Kim Clune, This One Wild Life

Publishers Cataloging In Publication

15 Great Pet Blogs And Their Most Memorable Posts / [Compiled and edited by] Kyla Duffy and Lowrey Mumford.

p. ; cm.

ISBN: 978-0-9833126-0-4

1. Pet Care. 2. Cats - Anecdotes. 3. Dogs – Anecdotes. 4. Animal welfare – United States. 5. Human-animal relationships – Anecdotes. I. Duffy, Kyla. II. Mumford, Lowrey. III. Title.

SF426.5 2011

Contents

Introduction: Why Do Pet Blogs Count?... 4

Bocci's Beef 9

Catladyland 20

Champion of My Heart.. 30

(DOG)SPIRED 39

FIDO Friendly.. 48

Grouchy Puppy Dog Days 55

Life with Dogs.. 63

Petfinder.. 68

Pet Health Care Gazette 74

Sebastian the Sensitive Soul 79

Speaking for Spot 85

This One Wild Life 93

Thoughts Fur Paws 102

Two Little Cavaliers.. 107

Woof Report 113

Bonus Blog: Happy Tails Books... 123

A Final Word.. 127

Introduction: Why Do Pet Blogs Count?

Pet blogs count because pets count. Let us clear up something else, right now. Pets are whichever animal you love in your home or domicile, be that a chicken, a lizard, a fish, or a dog, cat, bird…whatever. Pets come in all shapes and forms.

It's as simple as that. Pet bloggers are vocal advocates of pet causes, of pet health, pet heroes and pet humor. Evidence of their popularity can be seen at sites like I Can Has Cheezburger, Dogtime Media, Catster, Dogster, The Pet Podcast Channel and BlogPaws.

The rise of blogs as conversational tools naturally gave pet people the idea to begin blogging to share their stories and insights—with friends, family and anyone willing to click in. Over time, the connective nature of these budding relationships created dynamic communities that thrive on sharing.

People gravitate to pet stories and videos because they stir our emotions and bring a smile to our faces. In a world that is overflowing with negative news and stories of tragedy from sunup to sundown, pet blogs bring a breath of fresh air, revealing stories of happy reunions, funny antics, truly inspiring rescues, both the animal kind and the human kind, along with a multitude of photos, videos and poetic writing. It's true life commentary on society as a whole.

It's been said that a civilization is known by how it treats the "least" among its citizens. To pet people, pets are among the "least among us" and how they are treated reflects on the humanity of the people who care for them. Good or bad.

This is a primary reason people write pet blogs – to support those creatures who are so dependent upon care-givers.

When we decided to start BlogPaws, the online pet blogger community Caroline Golon, Tom Collins and I created in 2009, a lot of people looked at us with disbelief and said, "Pet bloggers? Why? How many can there be?"

First of all, we knew there were hundreds, maybe thousands, of pet bloggers. We knew they were eager to meet each other and to be connected online, via a community that would support efforts in shelter support, rescues, education on health and nutrition and provide a way to connect to brands that serve the pet industry. To those people who misjudge the human-animal bond, who think of pets as just animals tamed to provide companionship, launching a business that served pet bloggers (and their pets) seemed like a crazy idea – one that was certain to fail. To us, it seemed like heaven. To be able to read all those great blogs, look inside the hearts of those writers and show brands how to create the right kinds of products for our pets—it was a no-brainer.

And we were right. The pet blogging community is enormous. It's strong, vocal and determined, while at the same time being friendly, caring and joyful.

You will get a sense of that caring and determination in this book. There is more value here than all the money in Fort Knox. There is wisdom and inspiration, happiness and joy. There is laughter, followed by tears, followed by singing.

I predict that when you visit these blogs and take an hour or two to really enjoy them, one after another (perhaps over a period of several weeks), you'll become lifelong visitors. I predict that whether you consider yourself a pet parent or not, you'll recognize a bit of yourself in the musings of these blogs. I predict that you will look at the human-animal bond differently after you visit these blogs. You will finally feel the truth and the heart that each blogger brings to his or her words.

Mark Twain may have said it best: "I have been studying the traits and dispositions of the 'lower' animals (so called) and contrasting them with the traits and dispositions of man. I find the result humiliating to me." Pet bloggers came to the blogosphere knowing that. You'll leave each of these blogs having learned it.

Read and learn. Read and be entertained. Just read… you'll be glad you did.

Yvonne DiVita, BlogPaws co-founder

6

15 Great Pet Blogs

"The assumption that animals are without rights, and the illusion that our treatment of them has no moral significance, is a positively outrageous example of Western crudity and barbarity. Universal compassion is the only guarantee of morality." - Arthur Schopenhauer, German Philosopher

Bocci's Beefs

Behind the Blog:
Joan DeMartin

Can a human live a fulfilling life without a dog? That's the question Joan DeMartin faced after losing her Wire Fox Terrier, Carson, to old age. She soon found her answer at the local pound, when she locked eyes with a sweet terrier-mix. (Dogs and men with beards are Joan's genetic weakness). She brought home the exuberant pup for an afternoon trial visit, and when she saw how he loved, well, everything—her cat, Bella, her neighbors and playing fetch—they both knew that he was home. After soliciting names from everyone, including strangers on the street, she chose "Bocci" to honor her dog-loving, late Italian father, who had a passion for bocce ball.

Inspired By:
Bocci (adopted terrier-mix)

Doghouse:
Ohio

Little did Joan know that *Bocci* had literary talents in addition to his fetching abilities! They soon "collaborated" on a humor piece titled "Bocci's Beefs" for *Dog Fancy* magazine, in which Bocci complained bitterly about life with a cat, his failure to catch a squirrel and other sundry gripes about living with humans.

Bocci's writing talent, combined with Joan's career as a college writing instructor and freelance writer, made starting a blog a natural fit for both of them.

Within a few months of the debut of *Bocci's Beefs,* Joan and Bocci discovered, in an amazing confluence of serendipity, that a newly founded organization called *BlogPaws* was hosting its very first conference in their fair city. What they both learned from mingling with pet writers and pet product and service purveyors was that they all shared a passion for helping animals in need; they were kindred spirits.

From that moment on, Joan and Bocci decided to dedicate *Bocci's Beefs* to promoting pet adoption and rescue and to helping their readers understand the myriad issues facing companion animals in our society today: from debates about quality pet food and health care to conversations about the many forms of animal abuse, including an ongoing series about the relationship between dog auctions, puppy mills and pet stores. Joan and Bocci believe that blogging, combined with other forms of social media, is a powerful force to be harnessed and focused to speak for those creatures who cannot speak for themselves.

Favorite Posts:

Nuance
September 28, 2009

Can someone out there tell me how I'm supposed to know the difference between one of my (many) stuffed toys and oh, say, a black cashmere glove? They're all soft and furry, and believe me, they all taste the same. So how was I supposed to "know" that when Parental Unit dropped one of these so-called gloves (mistakenly, she claims) in my pile of toys laying on the floor, that I shouldn't run upstairs with it, stash it in my hiding place under the bed, and later chew it to shreds? And... how was I supposed to know that Parental Unit had (I'm embarrassed to admit this) stalked these gloves for months at Saks Fifth Avenue, waited till they went on sale, then set her alarm to get up early on the day after Christmas to buy these gloves at 30% off their already marked down price?

Look who's calling who crazy? She wandered around for weeks muttering to herself that they were the only "elbow length" gloves she'd ever owned. Who does she think she is, Cinderella, that she needs gloves up to her elbows? Something tells me she won't be going to a ball with a prince anytime soon. Hey, speaking of a ball...

All (Okay, Almost All) Kidding Aside
January 15, 2010

These last few days, it's been hard for me to talk just about all the stupid/funny stuff that humans do, because I can't help but think of the earthquake victims and survivors in Haiti. You know, I agree with Woody Allen, who said something like, "If someone in the world is starving, it ruins my whole day." The more I learn about the devastation in Haiti, the more down I get. If you can believe it, I couldn't even (fully) enjoy my biscuits yesterday! But there's one thing we all know can cure those blues—and that's to *help*, even in a small way. So here's a link to CNN, so you can find your way to help:

http://www.cnn.com/2010/LIVING/01/13/haiti.earthquake.how.to.help/index.html.

What really gave me the push to get this off my bleeding-heart chest was a "film" review I saw in *The Times* today (we in the Midwest call them "movies"). It's a documentary called *Mine*, by Geralyn Pezanoski, that "tells the story of the pets, mostly dogs and cats, left behind during the storm [Hurricane Katrina] when their humans were forced to flee." It got a darn good review (considering it was *The Times*) and is something that I'll see with a wad of tissues clutched in my paws. Here's the link to the review:

http://movies.nytimes.com/movie/457377/Mine/overview.

My First Time...Wearing Clothes?
October 24, 2009

I've always seen humans putting clothes on before they leave the house (in fact, Parental Unit spends so much time with her outfits and makeup just to take me for a walk, that I've started spinning in circles to pass the time), but I never dreamed that one day my turn would come.

Today, Parental Unit came home all giddy and flapping her jaw to her sister about what I'd be "wearing" to the Dog Parade tomorrow in the park. Well, I heard the word "park" and started to go for my leash, but what happened next was beyond even what I could concoct: She takes out this little jacket and scarf and starts "decorating" me like I'm a Christmas tree or something—putting my paws through the sleeves, fastening the snaps and tying and re-tying the scarf like I was on *Project Runway*. Then she put a big pair of goggles on my face (which I promptly removed—over and over) and finally declared me ready for the "contest" tomorrow. She said something about Amelia Earhart's dog...?

Okay, I'll put up with this just to make her happy—and because this thing's in the park. (Think I'll win anything with this getup?)

Let's Hear It for Us Mutts!
January 31, 2011

Or mixed breeds, or "blends" as Mike Arms, president of Helen Woodward Animal Center in San Diego, likes to call us. Whatever name you choose, there sure are a lot of us. And it seems, unfortunately, that somehow we end up in animal shelters. Go figure. According to statistics from http://www.muttigrees.org, an organization formed to help us mutts, "There are 50 million mixed breed dogs in the U.S. today, and three out of every four shelter dogs are mixed breeds." Yikes!

Now, we want this to be perfectly clear: we have nothing against purebred dogs. In fact, some of our best friends are purebreds (hehehe). And Parental Unit has always had purebred dogs in the past—until I came along, that is.

Of course, the idea these days is to get your purebred pooches from either rescue groups or responsible breeders, of which there are many. So, we love you, our purebred friends!

But there's another interesting angle to the story: it seems that, as the dogs go, so goes the country. In an article in yesterday's *New York Times* titled: "Black? White? Asian? More Young Americans Choose All of the Above," we learned that "blends" are all the rage among humans, too! According to this article, "The crop of students moving through college right now includes the largest group of mixed race people ever to come of age in the United States, and they are only the vanguard: the country is in the midst of a demographic shift driven by immigration and intermarriage." Read the full article at http://www.nytimes.com/2011/01/30/us/30mixed.html.

Now we happen to think this is a good thing. We love the idea of all sorts of ethnicities, religions, races (and dog breeds) uniting in marriage, procreation and whatever else they'd like to unite in. And it's high time that humans started emulating us dogs, which I'm sure is what's happening. I mean, we've been listening to you folks for centuries—the tables are finally turned!

And speaking of mutts, is this a face to love, or what?

Photo of me by Rachel Lauren Photography

A Young Dog Lover Worth Emulating
February 20, 2011

Remember last week when we promised to introduce you to a young lady who has found her calling? Well, Parental Unit and I were able to interview our friend, Meg, just yesterday, and we're thrilled to bring you excerpts from that interview today. Meg is the daughter of one of Parental Unit's friends, whom we know to be a long-time animal lover. And we also know that Meg has been shadowing a veterinarian, her chosen career, for more than four years. Now get this: Meg just turned 12, so that means she's been shadowing this vet since she was about seven or eight years old. (Parental Unit says she could probably say "Hello" pretty well at that age, but that's about it.)

Here's what Meg has to say about helping animals in need, becoming a veterinarian, and adding a new member to her family:

> **Parental Unit:** So, Meg, I hear you did something pretty special for your birthday celebration this year.
>
> **Meg:** I invited a few friends over for a party and decided to ask them to bring a small donation to the American Humane Society instead of bringing presents for me.
>
> **Parental Unit:** We think that's pretty nice of you, Meg! How much were you able to donate?
>
> **Meg:** We donated $250 to the Humane Society.
>
> **Bocci:** Whoa! $250 bucks! What a nice sum of money to donate. I'm sure they'll appreciate it.
>
> **Parental Unit:** What did your friends say about your unusual birthday request?
>
> **Meg:** My friends thought it was a great idea. They were excited to give!
>
> **Parental Unit:** I know that you want to be a veterinarian, and you've been shadowing a vet for quite a few years, Meg. What exactly do you do when you visit the clinic?

Meg: I go with the veterinarian and her staff when she sees each patient, help out when I'm asked, and usually just listen and learn a lot from the experience. I also get to observe during surgeries. I don't get freaked out by blood and all that other stuff.

Bocci: Blood? I'm starting to feel woozy...clunk!

Parental Unit: Just ignore Bocci; he'll be fine. Do you plan to help out any other animal organizations in the future?

Meg: I have a good friend who's interested in helping animals, too, and right now we're doing some research on puppy mills. We'll probably write letters [to raise awareness] when we get more information. And we're looking into more ways to raise money. We're probably going to expand into [more formal] fundraisers soon.

Bocci: O.K. I'm feeling better now—just had some water and a biscuit to normalize my blood sugar. Great about that fundraising thing, Meg. Just let me know when you get more ~~loot~~ money to donate. I've got just the ~~dog treats to buy~~ animal organization that would be grateful for your donation. Speaking of dogs, I hear you've got plans for a new addition to your household!

Meg: Yes, Bocci, this spring we're looking forward to bringing home a Wirehaired Pointing Griffon puppy!

Parental Unit: That's exciting. We'll look forward to visiting and taking lots of pictures!

Bocci: Oh boy, I can hardly wait to meet the little rascal! I'll be happy to pass on all the ways I've learned to strictly obey all of Parental Unit's commands.

Meg: Sure thing, Bocci!

P.S. Parental Unit and I can't help but wonder how many animals in need or other causes could benefit if more young folks would ask for a donation to a charity or cause instead of presents for just one birthday. We love this idea!

A hearty "thank you" to Meg and her family for allowing us to publish this inspiring interview. We'll leave you with a picture of Meg and her late dog, Kelley, whom they lost to old age last year.

An Interview with a Passionate Dog Activist
March 06, 2011

Here's the second in a trio of interviews with people who inspire us, and hopefully, will inspire you as well.

But as we all know, it's not enough to just be "inspired." You have to take that inspiration to the next level and actually *do something!* We all lead busy lives, so that's why Parental Unit and I are in favor of taking "baby steps." If you're inspired to help with a cause that you believe in, just do one small thing to benefit that cause. More on that later...

Now, we'd like to introduce you to a woman that Parental Unit met last fall at a Petapalooza fundraiser for a local humane society, Mary O'Connor-Shaver. As you'll see, Mary has done a lot more than take baby steps in her work to ban dog auctions and puppy mills in the great state of Ohio. Mary told Parental Unit and me that she's long been involved in dog rescue (visit http://www.columbustopdogs.com), but it all came together when she was invited by a friend in the dog rescue business to observe her first dog auction in 2006. (As you may know, dog rescue groups often go to dog auctions anonymously to buy the dogs and properly place them in loving homes.)

Mary (on the right) and a friend at last fall's fundraiser

Mary said that *she* was inspired to devote so much of her time to banning dog auctions and puppy mills because of the animal cruelty she witnessed first-hand at dog auctions and the corruption and consumer fraud she learned was rampant in the industry that was fed by those auctions.

The primary goal on her agenda these days is to collect enough signatures to bring an initiative, the Ohio Dog Auction Act, before Ohio voters in the fall of 2012. That initiative would ban dog auctions and raffles in Ohio. Ohio hosts the only dog auctions east of the Mississippi, where typically, buyers and sellers of dogs from 15 other states participate.

So what's so bad about dog auctions, you say? Dogs are considered property under current law in every state, and we've bought and sold them in one way or another for thousands of years. If there's one thing Mary wants my readers to understand, it is the connection among dog auctions, puppy mills, pet stores and the soaring overpopulation of abandoned dogs in the U.S., leading directly to the euthanizing of millions of dogs each year in overcrowded shelters across the country.

We'll give you the short version today and continue this informational series in posts to come. According to Mary, who is armed with extensive research, firsthand experience at dog auctions, and years of work with the state legislature, "Auctions are a major distribution channel for puppy mill breeders." That's where these alleged "breeders" dispose of the dogs who are no longer producing lucrative puppies and buy younger dogs to take their place. And most puppy mills, particularly the bigger operations, sell directly to pet stores, the biggest of which in our neck of the woods is Petland, the largest franchised pet store chain in the Midwest.

No reputable breeder sells their puppies to a pet store: they socialize their pups, test for genetic diseases, and require each new owner to sign a contract agreeing to spay or neuter the puppy and to return the puppy/dog *to the breeder* if it doesn't work out for the new owner for whatever reason and for the life of the dog.

Research also shows that pet store puppy purchases are made by "impulse buyers" who see a cute puppy in the window, especially around the winter holidays, and buy it right on the spot as a gift for a friend or family member. Perhaps it's a well-intentioned purchase, but if the new puppy just "doesn't work out," off it goes to the shelter, or worse, to the streets. That's the vicious cycle that Mary and all of her supporters in Ohio and neighboring states are working so hard to break.

Mary, (at left), working to educate

But let's get back to you, me and Parental Unit. How can we get involved and take those "baby steps" to help, no matter where we live? Here's what Mary says:

1. Visit her organization website and campaign page (http://www.banohiodogauctions.com) to learn more about these issues and how to get involved, and check out their Facebook page and show your support by becoming a "fan": http://www.facebook.com/group.php?gid=55644242409&v=wall.

2. After you educate yourself, talk with as many friends, family and co-workers about these issues as you can.

3. Find out what's going on in your state and get involved however you can.

As always, we appreciate your interest and your support, and we'd love to know how you feel about the issues we've raised.

Bocci's Beefs header artwork by Darrin Hoover

Bocci photos by Rachel Lauren Photography

Catladyland

Angie Bailey is a Minnesota writer, cat fancier, word game junkie, creative-project dabbler, music lover, food enthusiast, wife, and mother to two humans and three cats. She spends most of her days enjoying her family, blogging at Catladyland, writing for *Life with Cats*, playing Scrabble, laughing at her cats' shenanigans and finding the silliness in most everything.

Favorite Posts:

Stop, Drop and Sleep
October 7, 2010

I sometimes feel jealous that kitties can sleep most anywhere and succumb to the sandman at the drop of a cat. Seriously...have you ever met an insomniac cat? I know I haven't. How great would it be to just be able to stop, drop, and sleep? Hmmmmm......

Behind the Blog:
Angie Bailey

Inspired By:
Saffy, Cosmo, and Phoebe (rescue cats)

Kitty Condo:
Minnesota

Ahhh, the loaf position: tightly tucked and tuckered-out.

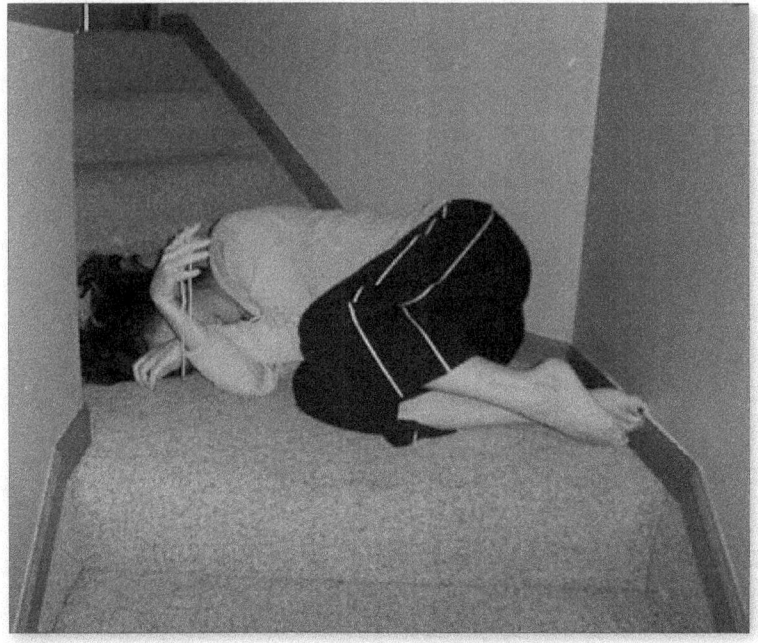

How nice to fall asleep on the stairs whilst in mid-play...

Paws warmed by the heat vent…how cozy!

Yes, sometimes I would definitely like to be able to sleep as comfortably and easily as a cat. But I must say that after looking at these photos, 1) It is clear that I really need to get back into yoga, and 2) I can't decide if these pictures look more like cute cat imitations or crime scene investigations.

Whiskered Wisdom
October 7, 2010

Sometimes I feel like I juggle a dozen things at once. When I feel overwhelmed with my ever-growing to-do list, I sometimes look to my cats to keep me grounded and moving in a slightly saner (or less insane, as it were) direction. These are some of their helpful reminders:

Take time for quiet meditation

Hugs and kisses are very important

Get in people's faces and ask for help

Remember to eat!

Sometimes it's ok to ask to be left alone

Thank goodness for my wise and helpful kitties. I shudder to think about the maniacal mess I'd be without them!

Off the Deep-End...Again
November 16, 2010

In previous posts, I've written about the silly images that give me giggles. I'm an expert daydreamer and self-proclaimed flake. Some people in my life find those qualities annoying because I'm easily distracted, but I happen to enjoy my little escapes. They are the least expensive sort of vacation and my luggage never gets lost.

Lately, I've been thinking about the places I'd like to take my cats, if they would be willing to go. I know these thoughts are far-out (and I'd never actually share them with my cats—they'd run for the hills), but it sends me into fits to imagine these scenarios and the looks on the faces of the people in said scenarios.

So here we go... Here comes another perilous plunge into the rabbit hole that is Angie's imagination. I hope you are wearing your padded bra and protective headgear...this may be a wild one!

I'd like to take...

...Saffy to the salon and tell the stylist she needs an up-do for the prom.

...Phoebe to the local elementary school and tell them I'm there to register her for kindergarten.

...Cosmo to the sports outlet and tell the salesperson he needs to be fitted for ice skates.

...Phoebe to IHOP and ask for a high chair, children's menu, and coloring sheet.

...Cosmo to Sylvan Learning Center and tell them he needs a tutor for geometry.

...Saffy to Williams-Sonoma and ask if they have a spatula that would fit into her tiny paw.

...Saffy to Target and tell them she is there to register for wedding gifts.

...Phoebe to Verizon and tell them we need to add her to our family plan.

...Cosmo to Taco Bell and ask to see the manager because he is there to apply for a job.

Am I the only one giggling at this? If so, that's just fine. I'm used to flying solo on my mini-vacations. If not, welcome aboard the crazy train. I'll save you a seat! Now I've gotta run... Cosmo is late to register for the SATs.

Your Friendly Neighborhood Catnip Dealer
December 23, 2010

Dear Mama
July 9, 2010

Dear Mama,

While you were at work this morning, I had a few thoughts, so I thought I'd write you a quick note before my next snooze.

1. Can you please quit folding the laundry and leave the warm, cozy clothes in the basket? I've never met a nap I didn't like, but fresh laundry napping is insane. Just sayin'.

2. When I follow you around the kitchen shouting at you, it means I want a snack. I don't care that I just had a snack five minutes earlier. I'm small and my stomach empties quickly. Thank you.

3. I miss nibbling through the wires on all of those stray pairs of earbuds I'd find lying around the house. What happened to them? Can you please buy more and leave a few pairs scattered about at whisker-level. Much appreciated.

4. Don't talk to me when I am going #2 in the litter box. That concentrated look of avoidance means I am busy. I will seek you out when I am finished with my business and we will converse at that time.

Thank you for your time and attention to the above requests. I look forward to your cheerful obedience.

Hugs,
Phoebe

http://championofmyheart.com/

Champion of my Heart

A real-time memoir set in the Colorado Rocky Mountains, *Champion of My Heart* is an award-winning dog blog featuring Lilly Elizabeth, a rescued Border Collie with crushing anxiety. Both comical and confusing, Lilly swings between extremes, cowering at the sight of a three-ring binder one minute, squaring off with a rattlesnake or other wildlife the next. Yep, life is never boring. Lilly once instigated a veterinary emergency after eating 130 paintballs. Two words: Technicolor. Vomit.

Adopter Roxanne Hawn struggles to help Lilly reach her potential. Amid many apparent failures, they find a shared calling.

Champion of My Heart is a blog about bravery and grace, compassion and perseverance. It details personal victories, even when life takes many unexpected turns. Offering insights on human relationships culled from situations

Behind the Blog:
Roxanne Hawn

Inspired By:
Lilly Elizabeth Hawn (rescued Border Collie)

Doghouse:
Colorado

only a smart, fearful dog can muster, *Champion of My Heart* delivers lessons for the real world.

A lifelong storyteller with a successful career in journalism and writing, blogger Roxanne Hawn is the winner of the 2010 DogTime Media Best Dog Blog Award and the 2010 Community Engagement Award from the Humane Society of Boulder Valley. She is the founder of Never Shock a Puppy, a humane dog training advocacy campaign.

Roxanne began writing about pets in 1995, when she worked for the American Animal Hospital Association and later for the American Humane Association. Roxanne served on the board of directors for the National Council on Pet Population Study and Policy (a coalition of animal welfare groups) and also volunteered for many years at an animal shelter, where she witnessed firsthand what happens when the human-animal bond breaks or never forms.

Since she started freelancing full time in 1999, many top dog magazines have published Roxanne's work, including *The Bark, Healthy Pet, Modern Dog, AKC Family Dog, AKC Gazette* and *Clean Run* (a dog agility magazine). She also writes for many pet industry trade magazines, including some in the veterinary profession.

In addition, Roxanne's other lifestyles work has been published by big-name publications such as *The New York Times,* Bankrate.com, *Natural Home, Reader's Digest,* and WebMD.

Roxanne and Lilly welcome new readers and fans as they strive toward their goal of publishing a full-blown memoir of life together.

Favorite Posts:

Five Ways a Fearful Dog Improves Your Life
March 24, 2011

Lilly, Roxanne's fearful dog

I sometimes wonder if I'd ever deliberately adopt a truly fearful dog again. Truth? I didn't know what I was getting myself into with Lilly when we adopted her in October 2004 from the Humane Society of Boulder Valley. Still, I cannot imagine missing all the amazing things she taught me about not just dogs and dog training/dog learning theory but also about life and love, relationships and finding (perhaps) my true calling.

Fearful dogs require work

It is, indeed, a lot of work to help Lilly cope in the world, starting with the tedious-but-necessary Relaxation Protocol that teaches dogs how good calm can feel. Living with a fearful dog is often a heartbreaking, frustrating, and slow exercise of daily life — with progress measured in the smallest possible increments. Yet, after reading some of the adoptable dog profiles I find online, I understand how lucky Lilly was to be rescued and quickly placed at such a young age (around 6 months old). Many other dogs currently in animal shelters and dog rescue groups face a much longer road ... sometimes years until they find the right forever home.

Consider adopting a fearful dog

So, in hopes of encouraging others to consider adopting fearful dogs or shy dogs, I offer this list of ways a fearful dog will:

- Improve your life
- Make you a better person
- Teach you important life lessons

Five ways a fearful dog improves your life

While Lilly will always be fearful, some 95% of the time she is perfectly happy and calm because we protect her from scary things and because we've taught her how to cope in the world.

1. **Fearful dogs teach you compassion...** because you often have daily, if not minute-by-minute, chances to recognize suffering and to do something to help.

2. **Fearful dogs hone your awareness and attention to detail ...** because it takes focus to find and understand what exactly your dog fears. You'll truly wake up to the world around you and realize just how much is happening every second. (Fair warning, you'll also suddenly find an untold amount of rude and/or clueless behavior... in that case, see number five.)

3. **Fearful dogs demonstrate the real meaning of trust...** because they don't just give it away for free. You must earn it every day not only with your good intentions but also through your actions, your words and yes, sometimes, your cheese. Not just in the beginning. Not just some days. Every day.

   Think about it like this. Do you know people who kind of treat their loved ones like crap most of the year, then make a big production of giving lavish gifts on certain holidays? Yeah, well... fearful dogs don't buy that kind of "love." They need, expect and deserve real love...

which in many cases involves tiny gestures all the time that other people won't even notice.

4. **Fearful dogs persevere, many times in the most unlikely situations…** and, that's a lesson people should internalize because most of the time the best things don't just magically happen without any effort. Keep at it (whatever "it" is for you) because your dog surely would.

5. **Fearful dogs teach perspective on ugly behaviors between people…** because when you understand what triggers set off your dog's fears, you also learn how to read even the most horrible behaviors between people for what they truly are. This gives you the chance to practice the dog training cue "leave it" in your own life.

What Dogs Can Teach Us: Leave It
October 5, 2010

We ask our dogs to "leave it" all the time. It's a handy dog-training cue that essentially means, "Let it go." Ignore that food on the ground. Stop fixating on that squirrel in the tree. Don't snark at that other dog. Yes, I know he's being rude, but keep on walking. We ask, and if we've done all the groundwork, our dogs often comply. They let it go. They move on.

The things that cause our dogs to react are just triggers, after all. They typically bode no real intent. "Leave it," we tell our dogs. It isn't real. It isn't scary. It isn't important… is what we mean. Focus on me, we promise, and everything will be fine.

Much like reactive dogs, reactive people lash out over some seemingly small trigger—be it a real or imagined transgression. Usually, the actual issue is something else entirely.

Once past threshold, as the research shows us, everyone around them goes on a rollercoaster ride of emotion.

Unleashed, that kind of fury cannot be called back.

Unlike most "dog fights," which often amount to little more than noise and movement, people do real damage with their words and through their actions. Sometimes what's said and what's done cannot be taken back. A snark is one thing. An unprovoked attack that reaches beyond the moment is another. It's true with dogs. It's true with people.

Irrevocable. That's the word for it. Irrevocable.

Being a trigger sucks. Cast in the role of villain in some drama I didn't even know existed, I now look to Lilly for guidance.

"Leave it," she tells me. "It isn't important."

I'm trying to believe her because so many times before she believed me.

Canine Gravity for Stressful Times
April 14, 2011

Pressures of modern life—be they related to work, families, political climate or global catastrophes—make a girl wish she could simply float away for a while and get a break from the grind. Yet, whether you face short, intense challenges or the death-by-a-million-cuts reality of lingering problems, the trick (as far as I can tell) is to stay put.

Now, I'm not going to try to fool you. My own emotional survival does require a certain amount of protection and distancing because, honestly, if I actually felt all the things I should be feeling about life right now, I'd never get out of bed.

I often take my cues on getting through daily life from the dogs:

Ginko faithfully pilots the sofa, serving as both witness and touchstone.

Lilly moves when I move, reacts when I react, providing a mirror for my own condition.

Dogs: Our anchor to what matters

Like a small, furry source of gravity, force of nature, the dogs ground me with their presence, through their humor, by the sheer force of needing to provide for them.

Sometimes, they do this by just being nearby. Other times, especially at night, Lilly chooses instead to curl up right on my chest or my tummy and hold me in place.

"Rest now, Mama," I pretend she tells me. "I'll hold you down so that you don't float away."

So, if you ever call me in the evening and I do not answer, it's because I have 35-pounds of love holding me in place.

Once Upon a Teeter
May 23, 2007

The one and only time Lilly did the competition-sized teeter-totter in agility training I nearly cried with joy. It was a fluke that's yet to be repeated. So, months of endless frustration followed those brief moments of happiness. Here's how it happened …

We popped by Biscuit Eaters, the agility training field we use in Boulder, Colorado, for a quick drop-in practice. Alone on the course, Lilly played with abandon. (Remember, she's fine alone but slow and totally fearful and shut down if other people and dogs are around. It's like training Dr. Jekyll and Mr. Hyde.)

So, we ran a few short sequences of agility obstacles, then played. Work, play. Work, play.

We rounded a turn, and I called "weave." My body must have told her something different because she blew off the weave poles and ran halfway up the big teeter-totter, which she typically gives wide berth – ever since another dog banged it in January 2005. (I've been screwed ever since. We hadn't introduced it yet, and it scared her to death.)

Lilly realized her mistake and ran back down toward me. She seemed really jazzed, though, so I thought what the heck. We circled back to pick up the weaves. She carried such speed out of the final pole that I called out, "Lilly, Teeter."

And, she flew. No hesitation. No worry. No pause at the middle. Just sprint, tip, bang. Lilly even held her two-on, two-off contact – with her front feet on the ground and her rear feet still touching the teeter-totter.

I started praising her like mad, dropped to my knees, and opened her jackpot bowl. I let her eat every morsel of food inside.

She seemed thrilled with herself for about three heartbeats. Thump-thump, thump-thump, thump-thump. Then, she freaked, realizing what she'd done (I guess).

She tucked tail and slunk off to hide near her toy bag along the fence. Moment over.

I cajoled her into playing some more and tried again later, but no luck. Refusal.

So, I jacked the adjustable teeter-totter up to near-full height and tried that instead. Run, tip, bang. Perfect. Over and over. So, the day wasn't a total loss. Then again, she's been doing the adjustable one for more than a year.

I know a lot of other people wish their dogs thought more, made better decisions on the agility course. I have the opposite problem. My sweetie girl thinks too much, worries too much. (She's a lot like me.)

But, for that one moment, she forgot everything and ran.

(DOG)SPIRED

(DOG)SPIRED strives to increase public awareness about dog-related issues. The topics of the blog are varied. For example, it includes information about dog facts, recent news about dogs, and personal accounts of people who own or rescue dogs.

For more than two years, the (DOG)SPIRED blog has taken readers on a voyage into the world of dogs and the love we all share for our canine friends. It has a fabulous team of writers and editors, which are led by the chief editor, Leslie Brown. Leslie believes that dog rescue and adoption are key to animal welfare, and she is involved in promoting forever homes for dogs that are injured or neglected.

Doghouse: Washington

Get your very own "Why Buy? Rescue a Dog" t-shirt, along with other great doggy items, at our store. Enter **HAPPYTAILS** as your coupon at checkout for 20% off your first order.

Favorite Posts:

Why Adoption is the Best Option
By MissionPETS on January 12, 2011

Why adopt?

1. Adoption means saving a life. As sad as it sounds, nearly four million animals in shelters across the United States are euthanized each year, simply because there are not enough homes for them. Too many people give up their dogs, don't spay or neuter them or buy them from pet stores, while too few people adopt from shelters or rescue groups. Shelters have a limited amount of space, and when they need more room, dogs who have been there for awhile are euthanized to make room for new dogs—and more arrive every day. When you adopt a dog, you are actually saving two lives. You are saving the life of the dog you take home, and you are freeing up a spot for a new dog to be rescued.

2. You will save money. Many of us know that, financially, times are tough these days. Buying a dog from a breeder or pet store can cost upwards of a thousand dollars. Adopting a dog is significantly cheaper. Adoption fees typically run between $60 and $300, and dogs from reputable organizations will be vaccinated and spayed/neutered prior to going home with you. You'll spend more than that on vet bills, in

addition to the purchase price, if you buy a dog from a breeder or pet store. Your adoption fee will also include advice and guidance from a rescue worker or shelter staff.

3. Purebreds galore! Many people don't realize that as many as one in four dogs in shelters or rescue groups are purebred. How could this be, you may ask. Sometimes when people buy purebred dogs, they are "impulse" buyers. A family might think a dog is cute and take him home, not realizing how much care and attention he needs. Or, the novelty wears off, and they no longer want the puppy when he gets bigger. Sometimes, people lose their homes, end up in a divorce, have babies, or move into an apartment complex that won't take dogs. There are many reasons why purebreds end up in shelters, and most of them are a result of problems related to the people, not the dogs.

4. Shelters offer variety and customer service. Animal shelters and rescue groups have a wide variety of animals to choose from. Shelter staff can usually give you some information about a dog's background and temperament, and with their help, you can even spend some time with him prior to adopting. This will help you make a decision about which dog is right for you, your family, and your lifestyle.

5. Pet shop puppies come from puppy mills. When you adopt, you are saying "no" to puppy mills. Puppy mills are "factory" breeding facilities that put profit above animal welfare. Most dogs raised in these facilities are kept in very poor conditions with little-to-no medical care or human interaction, and they are confined to very small cages as long as they live. They are bred over and over again, and when they are no longer profitable, they are discarded: killed, abandoned, or sold at auctions. The puppies in these facilities are sold in pet stores, through the Internet, or in newspaper ads. They target whoever is willing to pay, and the buyers don't suspect a thing is wrong. The pups are said to have come from great "breeders," yet buyers never get to see the facilities that the pups come from. Many puppy-mill puppies have health problems that may not show for months. Buying a puppy from a pet shop supports this cruel industry. Adopting a dog rather than buying one ensures that you are not supporting puppy mills. The more people who adopt, the less people buy from puppy mills, and hopefully, these

facilities will eventually stop operating altogether. Your local shelter or rescue group has many great dogs—healthy and well socialized—who need you as much as you need them.

6. Adoption equals helping pet overpopulation. Every year millions of dogs are euthanized because of overpopulation. There are just too many dogs and not enough "forever" homes. By adopting your new best friend, you are helping to reduce overpopulation. Your adoption fee covers vaccinations and medical procedures for your dog and goes toward saving other dogs' lives, providing humane education, and running the shelter.

7. Rescue dogs make loving companions. Some rescue dogs have been abandoned; some were victims of family issues or neglect and cruelty; and some never had a home of their own. All of them yearn for a fur-ever family to love them unconditionally. Many of these dogs are well-mannered and have already been housetrained. Adult dogs make wonderful companions. They might not need to be trained, they sleep all night, and they already know the lay of the land.

8. Dogs bring cheer. After carefully researching the right dog for your home and lifestyle, and with some help from your local shelter or rescue group, bringing home a new fur friend will brighten up your life! Dogs have been proven not only to offer unconditional love, but to help us on a therapeutic level. Dogs help us smile, relax, and enjoy each day. They help us to feel fulfilled, and we care for them in return. They can lift up our spirits and relieve loneliness. Dogs can also encourage us to exercise! The physical activity associated with caring for a dog has health benefits such as lowering blood pressure, strengthening the heart, and improving blood circulation. Dogs are mostly healthy–and they are fun, too. They'll add a little warmth, spunk, and love to your home.

There are loving dogs in all shapes and sizes available for adoption from your local shelter and rescue groups, and they all await a home to call their own. Serving as canine companions is their job, while yours is to find one of your own and bring him (or her) home, so that he can have a new chance at life. Adopt your new fur-friend and save a life.

Top 10 Signs You Are a Dog Lover
By Sniff Seattle on April 10, 2011

There are dog lovers, and then there are *dog lovers*. Which one are you? Here's a list of the "Top 10 Signs You Are a Dog Lover."

#10 Most days you have a "glistening" on your face from dried doggy kisses.

#9 You haven't seen your own doctor in years. But the vet? Last week!

#8 You make a point to sit scrunched in the corner of the couch so your dog can be comfortable.

#7 You reach into your pocket hoping to find a breath mint. But, no. It's a doggy treat.

#6 No matter how hot or extremely cold it is, you roll down the car window, so your furry friend can hang his head out.

#5 Your best conversations are with your dog.

#4 There are about 32 squeaky toys laying around your house.

#3 You sleep crowded on the corner of the bed and would probably go to the floor if you had to so your dog could get a good night's sleep.

#2 You're covered with almost as much dog hair as your dog! And, you don't think twice about it.

#1 You're still wearing sweatpants from your college days. Your dog? Cute *new* sweater!

10 Reasons to Foster a Dog
By Leslie Brown on June 18, 2010

To make a real impact on homeless animals, consider becoming a foster parent. Providing a temporary home for a dog in need is a very important and rewarding experience. Here are 10 reasons why you should consider taking a foster dog into your home to become part of your family.

1. In animal rescue, a foster home is a necessary ingredient for moving a dog out of a shelter and on the way to a good forever home.

2. Some dogs don't do well in a shelter environment. They may be elderly or frightened of the smells and sounds. These dogs have a much greater chance of being adopted if they're placed in a home environment and are given some TLC.

3. If a foster dog needs veterinary care, it is the responsibility of the particular shelter to provide it. Some shelters can even provide food and other supplies to their foster homes.

4. Fostering a dog can be a rewarding experience for anyone of any age. As long as you are allowed to have pets, you can enjoy the companionship of a dog who needs a temporary home.

5. As you spend time with your foster dog, you can learn about canine behavior, grooming, and social interactions.

6. You'll learn the finer points about the dog's personality. This is a wonderful gift you can give to people looking to adopt the dog. You'll be able to inform them of all the dog's strong points as well as areas that need to be focused on if they are considering adopting your foster dog.

7. If you already have a dog, fostering can provide your pup with a companion and playmate.

8. Fostering a dog teaches children about compassion and generosity.

9. Fostering means that you save a life. You are making room for another dog at the shelter. One more open run or kennel means one less dog put to sleep.

10. Having a foster dog lets you actively participate in the rehabilitation of a traumatized or needy dog. Due to the attention and security you give him in your home, your foster can become a different dog—less timid and less emotionally or physically injured.

Most of all, fostering is incredibly satisfying. The day your foster dog finds his perfect forever home might be a sad one for you, but know that he wouldn't be where he is without all of your efforts and affection!

Barney and the Shopping Cart
By James Henerson on May 11, 2010

At this moment, my dog Barney is lying by my desk, looking up at me with that, "Why aren't you taking me for a walk?" look in his big, fur-fringed brown eyes. It's a habitual glance, and it never fails to stir just enough guilt so that, more often than not, I stop what I'm doing and take him for a walk. Little does he know that on this occasion I'm writing about just that, a walk taken 4½ years ago.

Barney, or Barnes, Barnaby, Barnacles, or occasionally Poodle Paws, (depending on how whimsical I'm feeling), was my six-month-old, 50-pound puppy when I succumbed to one of those looks and consequently hooked on his leash. With his behind wriggling and his tail waving, we set out for Whole Foods, our local supermarket, some six blocks away in Sherman Oaks, California. With frequent stops for sniffing, marking, and once for a pooh stop, we made our way down my steep, curving driveway onto Kingswood Lane. We then made a quick right turn onto Woodcliff, which is a hillside route to the west side of Los Angeles for those wanting to avoid the 405 freeway (frequently a parking lot). We made another quick right onto Saugus, which crosses Valley Vista, and on past Sutton and Greenleaf into the Whole Foods parking lot.

I tied Barney to a shopping cart with his leash, told him to stay, and hurried into the market. In defense of Barney's future actions, I must admit that at six months old, the doggie equivalent of a toddler, the command "Stay!" was not yet in his repertoire.

Before I could head for the check-out stand, a voice came over the loudspeaker. "Will the owner of a tan shaggy dog please come to the entrance?" A stab of instant fear. Oh my God, he's been run down in the parking lot! The checker pointed. "He went that way!"

"That way" lay Sepulveda Boulevard, a major north-south highway, always crowded with speed-limit testing traffic. Fear transformed instantly into panic. I ran to Sepulveda, dashed 20 paces in one direction, 20 in the opposite. No Barney, but a shopper who had just parked in the Whole Foods lot pointed toward Saugus, mercifully away from Sepulveda. "I think he went that way."

With my heart pumping and the adrenaline flowing, I sped up Saugus until I could see the end. No Barney, but there were several streets leading off from Saugus to the left. He could have decided to take any one of them. I was immobilized. What to do?

I made a command decision. Run home, pick up my car, and canvass the neighborhood. At warp speed, I sprinted the last four blocks, arriving at the foot of my driveway near to cardiac arrest. Exhausted, palms on my thighs, girding myself for the final ascent, I heard a galvanizing sound: woof.

And there, sitting in front of the entrance to the house, still attached to the Whole Foods' shopping cart, having dragged it six long blocks through four unfamiliar turns, and up a steep driveway, the expression in his eyes said something like "Where the heck have you been? I've been waiting here for hours." It was Barney, the intrepid dog with the internal GPS. Lassie, eat your heart out!

http://fidofriendly.com/

FIDO Friendly

Doghouse: Idaho

FIDO Friendly is the only magazine dedicated to the travel and lifestyle of man's best friend, and the one magazine your dog will thank you for. The *FIDO Friendly* blog is an extension of the magazine, which conveys a love of all things dog and is now entering its 11th year in print. Both the blog and magazine share the very latest hotel and destination reviews along with health and wellness topics, dog training advice, rescue and feel-good stories, contests and information about the latest pooch products to hit the market.

The key dog-lovers behind the blog and magazine are Susan Sims (Publisher), Nicholas Sveslosky (Editor in Chief), and Carol Bryant (Social Media Director and Writer/Blogger). In addition to writing for *FIDO Friendly*, Carol Bryant is a frequent media contributor, having appeared on Animal Radio and Oprah Radio's Gayle King Show, WBAL-TV, and News12CT. She also serves as a guest speaker at conferences and seminars about dogs and dog travel.

Favorite Posts:

Anatomy of a Grieving Dog Mom
By Carol Bryant on July 28, 2010

"There's a hole in my heart where whole used to be." Those were the first words that came to mind when I sat down today to write this piece about grief, the power it spews into one's life whether we want it or not. The great Emily Dickinson wrote so many passages about death, yet one resonates over and over: "Forever is composed of nows." It certainly is. Are you loving someone today? Missing someone today? Wanting something today? Right now, you hold the forever that is the feeling. Right now.

And today, now, my forever is grief.

It's an odd thing, grief. We fear it, dismiss it, try and avoid it, occasionally have brushes with it, and most often times without warning, it invites itself into our lives. No welcome mat, but it comes nonetheless. Good ole' Emily said it best: "Because I could not stop for death, He kindly stopped for me." So when Lucy Maloney asked if she could have the honor of immortalizing my Brandy Noel in replica form with one of her miniatures, I hesitated.

Did I want those feelings to resurface? Would people think I was "weird" for wanting to have this forever keepsake? Would this set me back to day one, when I let go of my baby girl's frail, disease-ravaged body, so it was free to soar and I was left alone without her physical presence? None of that mattered, I deduced. This is a gift for me. Some of us visit cemeteries. Some light a candle in memory of, while others suffer in silence because, after all, "It's just an animal." Nod your head if somewhere along life's highway you've had that comment thwarted your way.

There's no wrong way to grieve, my grief counselor told me. "You saw a grief counselor because your dog died?" Uh, okayyyyy. Yep, some people validate themselves and their ability to master the art of grieving by tossing eye rolls and handing out sneers like napkins at a cocktail party. <thumps hand to forehead> Oh, wait, that's right. Anger is a part of the process. Some wounds run deep.

So I sent a locket of hair to Lucy Maloney with some photographs of a life well lived and forever painfully missed. It costs two postage stamps to send grief these days. Not bad. I figured I would see something resembling my Brandy in microscopic, thimble-sized form come back to me, where I'd keep it in a closet until the day came I could face her likeness without melting into a puddle of hurt.

What did arrive changed me. Me, who knows all about grief, has mastered the art of suffering through it, and while not kicking its choke hold on me, overcame it and carries it with her like a shield of sorts. A wounded warrior. The mailman delivered hope. Hope costs a few more than two stamps, by the way.

I called a family member to come open the box for me. Same as the day I had to let my baby go at the vet. Please don't make me do this alone.

What surfaced was nothing short of a complete likeness of my Brandy Noel. Her fur intertwined with the process Lucy uses to make miracles come to life. She stands more than several inches high; she certainly isn't thimble-sized, but the gaze in her eyes, the ever so slight tilt of her head, the love in who she always shall be, those are the magical qualities in Lucy Maloney's work that were brought to life. Many a tear fell that day and continue to do so. It's my grief, after all.

"Are you going to sleep with it? Put it next to her ashes?" These are some things people asked me. Contrary to popular belief, no, I'm not sitting home with an Ouija board summoning her spirit, nor am I immortalizing her with a dedicatory wing of the house. But even if I were, am I not a fully functioning adult? Don't I pay taxes and live and laugh, earn an income and rescue stray dogs? Don't I have the right as a human being to hurt and deal as I see fit? What is wrong with this world to diminish the handling of one's grief?

My Brandy is home in the closest sense possible until again we meet. Lucy Maloney is a maker of miracles and far above the craft her hands create. She is sort of a Clarence to George Bailey. Well, at least to me. For that, I am forever indebted.

As for my hurt, if you've loved and lost someone, you are walking that path with me. I view my grief as a suitcase. Some days it's merely an overflowing cosmetics bag, and others it's Samsonite gorilla-sized. Sometimes I feel like I'm on a carousel in the airport waiting for the form my grief will take. Do I wait days or weeks before I tear up and ache so very much, or is today a carry-on kind of day, where I just take it with me? In any event, I know my luggage always arrives and never gets lost. I've learned losing a loved one means gaining a new identity. Victim of grief, survivor of hurt and eventually, carrier of pain.

I was one of those people, by the way, who said, "Never again. I cannot get this close to an animal like this." But now he sits at my feet daily, and his name is Dexter, by the way. My never again. Thankfully, I think with my heart and then ask my brain to double check my work. I could never not love this way again.

Will you like Lucy Maloney's work should you choose to have her create magic for you? More than words could say, yes. Celebrating the life of a dog with a forever full of nows, that's the uniqueness of what Lucy does. "It came to me that every time I lose a dog, they take a piece of my heart with them. And every new dog that comes into my life gifts me with a piece of his or her heart. If I live long enough, all the components of my heart will be a dog, and I will become as generous and loving as they." Anonymous wrote that. I bet they've grieved a suitcase-full, too.

Lucy Malony Miniatures Website: http://miniature-dogs-cats.com/shop/

Skiing Handicapped Dog: From Pound Puppy to Powderhound

By Carol Bryant on June 13, 2010

Just call him Codski.

"There's no sense in throwing a life away." When Zane and Val Henning of Wasilla, Alaska, see their Cocker Spaniel, Cody, trail-blazing through the snow, this thought resonates. Cody entered the couple's lives in the fall of 2005. "He was in terrible shape with half a left ear, a huge scar over his head and part of his left eyelid missing," said Zane Henning. "We adopted him, had his health problems addressed, cleaned him up, and he became a completely different dog."

With an uphill battle behind, the future looked bright. And then Cody ate. "Cody was so starved. He ate the same amount as our other two Cockers, but due to his emaciated condition, the onset of weight was rapid," Zane remarked. Cody did more than tip the scales; the sudden accumulation of weight to his small proportion created an unusual inward curving of the back, resulting herniated disk.

The couple received news every Fido-guardian dreads: Cody's condition made it best to put him down. With a 10-percent chance that Cody would ever walk again, the Hennings refused and sought other options.

"Although Cody spent a week in therapy, his back end was paralyzed. All we have to do is express his bladder for him," Zane stated. How would an environmental coordinator and a stay-at-home Cocker mom manage trudging through the Alaskan snows with two able-bodied dogs and one with a physical limitation? Although wheelchairs for Fido facilitate dry ground mobility, the heavy snows of Alaska present challenges.

Not for Cody.

In the fall of 2009 while out on a walk, Zane noticed a skier pass by. He explained, "In the deep snow, ski poles create potholes, so Cody's wheelchair got stuck. I purchased a set of used skis at a local thrift store for five dollars. I cut the tips off, made small wooden blocks so the wheels could sit into them, screwed the skis on and nailed everything together. I used bungee cords to set the wheels in and pinch them between. Everything stays in place."

These days, the only downhills in Cody's life are the trails he takes on every day. Cody is a natural in his affectionately termed "ski-el-chair." Zane beams, "The first time he started tearing around corners with no resistance, he was free to run." Val reports the only downside is trying to keep up with Cody. They do a walk/run three miles a day, so sometimes she leashes him.

From pound puppy to powderhound, Cody houses an Olympic-style spirit in a Cocker-sized body. No sense in throwing a life away, not when Cody has miles to go and slopes to conquer.

Get Your Licks on Route 66
By Susan Sims on October 7, 2010

It was a dreary day in Los Angeles, but our 42-foot climate-controlled adoption bus was set up in the parking lot at Griffith Park, and Animal Radio had come out to broadcast on the final day of our month-long pet adoption tour, Get Your Licks on Route 66.

The stories of those who came to adopt that final day were different, but their hearts were all in the same place.

A retired couple had stopped at Griffith Park during an RV trip, looking to find Jay Leno tickets. They saw our buses and decided to take a look at what was going on. Two ladies were smitten by a Chihuahua-mix labeled Barry. Two hours later they came back with their husbands and adopted this lucky fellow. They determined that Barry, now called Griffith (after the park), would make a perfect addition to their home on wheels that already included one dog and four cats.

A family of four always wanted a Beagle and had waited for their kids to be of a certain age to help take care of an additional family member. As luck would have it, a Beagle-mix was waiting for them on the adoption bus that day.

A young girl fell in love with a white Terrier-mix and was just in time. The dog had been at the shelter for three weeks; his life would have ended the following week if his guardian angel had not stopped by that day.

Volunteers took turns walking each dog, showcasing their talents to would-be adopters. Truly a labor of love for these individuals, many who had the reluctant task of bringing the pets that were not adopted that day back to the shelter.

The best thing about adoption day, beyond placing pets into new forever homes, is the fact that many people who visit that day will go home, "sleep on it," and return the next day to adopt. After all, it is a lifetime commitment—one not to take lightly.

In the end, 282 pets found new forever homes on our month-long pet adoption tour. It's a small dent in the grand scheme of things, but it's a start.

We are already planning for next year. If you happen to live in a city near historic Route 66, keep an eye out for our adoption bus rambling down America's Favorite Highway. It would be great to see you at one of our events.

Grouchy Puppy Dog Days

Behind the Blog:
Sharon Castellanos

Inspired By:
Cleo (adopted Shepherd/Husky mix)

Doghouse:
California

Sharon Castellanos began writing the Grouchy Puppy Dog Days blog to educate and entertain dog lovers through interviews and stories written from her unique perspective. The blog is based on the following fundamental beliefs:

- Dogs make us human. By allowing ourselves to learn from dogs, we can become closer to our own humanity.
- Dogs give fearlessly. When people recognize their unconditional companionship and loyalty, the benefits are endless.
- Dogs are amazing creatures whose very nature gives us the opportunity to improve our own outlook on life every day.
- Sharing positive and inspiring stories about life with a dog provides an important cosmic counter balance to the dark side of animal welfare.

- Focusing on those who are making a difference in the animal world allows readers to learn how our actions, big or small, can have a positive impact on the world.

Favorite Posts:

Dog Household Tips: Ways We can Help our Dogs as They Age
January 21, 2011

According to a 1998 Gallup Organization survey, pet owners regard their animals not only as part of the family, but also as better companions than some human members of their family.

This survey might be more than 10 years old, but its truth rings even more loudly today. We approach the care of our beloved pets with the same intensity and commitment as we provide our human family members.

I started to write this post about my dog Cleo and how as a senior dog now she courageously tackles three flights of stairs every day.

Rather than focus strictly on applauding my dog, like a proud parent at a track meet or science fair, I decided to step back and instead, share the advice and tips that I've learned. Having a household with an aging pet takes some adjustment, but the reward of being with a happy and contented dog is totally worth it.

Bragging about Cleo's intelligence is fun, don't get me wrong, but I'd rather share real ways we have worked with Cleo in the hope that it helps others. At the end of this post I will share several links to senior dog blogs and other resources for senior dog health.

First things first: Changes. Look out for any changes because dogs, especially older ones, are all about the routine. Cleo knows when it is dinner time or breakfast time before I do sometimes. Her afternoon walk missed? Forget about it! If she were to not be interested in food or in going out for her morning pee break, that would set off red flags for me. Be observant of any changes: behavior, weight, activity, eating or bathroom habits are all areas to watch. If you catch something early on, that particular vet visit could mean everything to your dog's health.

Since dogs cannot hold onto a handrail like a human does, we discovered these tricks made all the difference to Cleo's confidence on the stairs.

Light. Having a well-lit stairwell helps her initial steps at each landing.

Carpet treads. Our stairs are hardwood and this 85-pound dog with long legs but little kitten feet, slipped and scratched her way up and down them for months. We could see it was only a matter of time before she became fearful of the stairwell. In the photo you can see small green carpets that look nice while quickly restoring Cleo's confidence. They are easy to pick up and vacuum, too.

Lead the way. We guide Cleo down the stairs by always going first, and staying one step ahead of her. If it is in the evening and she is tired, we turn the lights up bright and tap the first step with our hands sharply to help her senior vision. This focuses her attention and nose, before she eases herself down the rest of the way following along the walls.

Old dogs can't jump. Besides the carpet treads, we have also found dog beds for Cleo that are made for the older dog. Last year we started discouraging her from jumping onto the couch and our bed, as much as we wanted her there with us. We have more than one dog bed, so Cleo has one to nap in and can be off the wooden floor, even when the other has its cover in the wash. If your dog is short, you still may need to get a ramp to help them for certain tasks. Our car isn't very tall, and with her long legs Cleo doesn't need a ramp to "walk" into the back.

Grooming parties. Besides keeping your dog looking pretty, even with a graying muzzle, regular brushing allows you to give Fido the once over. Cleo still loves a good brushing even if she only tolerates her nails being filed. What is important though, is that by regularly grooming your dog, any lumps or bumps, hair loss, hot spots, discolorations, etc. will be detected and that gives you a chance to get your dog to the vet—pronto. Early detection for humans and dogs is always better.

The following are useful senior dog resources that can be found online, but you should always check in with your own veterinarian:

- Petfinder: Caring for your Senior Dog
- American Animal Hospital Association (AAHA) Senior Pet Care
- *Whole Dog Journal*: Senior dogs hearing loss

Dog Lovers Meet Here: 10 Reasons Why
November 8, 2010

Dog owner. Pet parent. Animal nut. Most people I've run across associate themselves with one of these labels. It seems that dog and pet people put themselves on a responsibility scale that moves from wild abandon to strict domination.

However you self-identify, I consider myself a moderate dog lover more than anything, and I'll tell you why.

Dog training is important, but I admit that I'll never put the same amount of time my mother, a former professional dog trainer, did with our purebred show dogs.

I work hard to give my dog a good diet based on her age, lifestyle, size and mobility, even if it means cooking her meals.

Because I want people to know we have a big dog in the house, I will let her bark at noises. Loudly.

When we go for walks I pick up her poop, sometimes in pink biodegradable bags.

If we meet people or other dogs on her walks, I will keep her leash short and guide her away if neither human nor dog want to interact with us.

Every morning I clean the goop out of her eyes and thank her for letting me up close to her face with my morning breath.

I buy the jumbo-sized Neosporin and hydrogen peroxide because we use it regularly for our cuts as well as for her dog scrapes.

Though my city is terrible at enforcement, I gladly pay for her vaccinations and a dog license each year.

We make arrangements for her to stay with friends rather than take her on trips because while we want her with us, we know she does not like riding in the car.

She never stops loving us. The least I can do is carefully keep the warm sudsy water out of her eyes when we bathe her.

All the ways I care for my dog are part of my job. Isn't it my duty to pick up my dog's poop? Shouldn't you give your dog the kind of food that makes him or her healthy?

I love being in charge of Cleo. Having her rely on me is a wonderful vote of confidence as a human. Common sense hasn't let me down yet, and with Cleo's ability to trust us, our family should be just fine with dog lovers at the helm.

How Do You Know If and When to Add to Your Pack?
August 10, 2010

We live in a big city. This meant at the top of our initial list of questions was, "What is the right size and energy level dog for us?" Once we decided on that, we agreed that we would wait until we had the right-sized home and lifestyle to accommodate this future dog. We waited nine years before adopting Cleo from the San Francisco SPCA.

How do you know if and when to add to your pack?

We have had Cleo for five years now, and she is about seven years or older. I've started thinking about whether it would be a good idea to get a second dog. Our big girl loves little dogs and puppies and could make a great matriarch. And I admit that as "an only child" she could use more regular canine interaction than what she gets now.

Cleo has become a bit spoiled, with my giving in to her demanding affection and attention out of guilt as much as from my own love of spending time with her. Is another dog the answer, or would Cleo be better served if she had more mental exercise? Searching for answers, I found Patricia McConnell, a certified applied animal behaviorist, dog trainer and author of two books: *The Other End of the Leash: Why We Do What We Do Around Dogs*, and *For the Love of a Dog: Understanding Emotions in You and Your Best Friend*.

She wrote a great post on her own website titled, *How Much is Enough?* on how much training and attention our dogs need every day. It got me wondering if Cleo's skin issues might be related to her not getting enough mental and physical exercise. We walk her every day for 30 minutes, and she goes out with a playgroup of about five dogs twice a week for two hours. Does she have behavioral issues that are manifesting themselves through the itching and biting? My guilty conscience points the finger squarely at myself, and that as the human, all of Cleo's problems stem from my inability to take care of her properly.

Have I become Cleo's enabler?

I wonder if at this age how much behavior modification I realistically can expect from her. And from me, would I be up to that possibly complex task? While we wait for the blood test results from the vet on what, if anything, she is allergic to, I vacuum every two days all the hair that she naturally sheds or purposefully scratches off whenever alone.

Part of me would like to get a second dog.

The dog could be a playmate for Cleo, solving all of our problems at once—for the modest cost of adoption fees and additional food. Problem solved, right? Somehow I don't quite believe it. The logic reminds me of troubled marriages where the couple decides that bringing a baby into the situation will solve every issue between the two of them.

Is now the right time to add another dog to our pack?

The more I think about it, the more time I know we need before we make any decision. After the reading I have done, we need to explore first this issue of exercise and wait to see what the test results tell us. Making changes to our behavior as much as hers is where I plan to start.

Adopting Cleo from the San Francisco SPCA was the best experience ever.

I can't imagine ever buying a dog again. Whatever the future holds, one decision that will remain the easiest is our choice to adopt rather than buy a dog.

*Photo credit: Sharon Castellanos

http://www.lifewithdogs.tv

Life with Dogs

Neil Brogan is immersed in technology by day as the VP of marketing for an IT consulting firm. By night he's hard at work as the editor of Life With Dogs, a busy, growing, general interest dog site with a focus on dog news and video.

He, his wife and their three dogs reside in northern Vermont, where they spend weekends exploring the rural countryside between blogging shifts. They recently celebrated a milestone, reaching the 50,000 fan mark on their Facebook page. Lovers of all creatures, Neil and his wife are well known supporters of Greyhound and other dog rescue efforts.

Favorite Posts:

Old Friends
October 26, 2009

An old friend contacted me recently. We had fallen out of touch after our last move many years ago. I recently logged in to Facebook to

Behind the Blog:
Neil Brogan

Inspired By:
Nigel Buggers (rescued Greyhound)

Doghouse:
Vermont

find a friend request for Nigel from a dog with a very familiar last name. Curiosity piqued, I immediately accepted and jumped to the profile of this dog to verify what I had suspected. I found my way to contact info, and within minutes this old friend and I were chattering away, catching up on all things dog. The time and circumstance that had separated us fell by the wayside as she described the events that led to our reunion.

Some of you will recall an old post, specifically this Wordless Wednesday post (above photo) of a Nigel-looking Greyhound pouncing or perhaps running. I let that post linger for the entire day before divulging that the dog pictured was not actually Nigel, but was in fact his very similar looking cousin, Ferrin. Ferrin was adopted by this old friend shortly after she met Nigel and fell in love with Greyhounds.

Not too long ago, our old friend was walking Ferrin on the bike path that winds through Burlington and along the shores of Lake Champlain. In all but the most severe weather, the bike path is a fairly happening place, with throngs of joggers, skaters, bikers and dog walkers scuttling about. On this particular evening, our old friend was accosted by one of the bike path walkers, who took one look at Ferrin and stopped in her tracks immediately. Our old friend looked up just in time to see this stranger approaching, excited and smiling. Before she could even say hello, a question was fired at her: "Oh my God, is that Nigel Buggers from Facebook?"

My friend politely explained that Ferrin was not Nigel, and after a brief exchange, old friend and random bike path exerciser went their separate ways. She could not help but wonder why a stranger was so excited to find one Nigel Buggers cavorting about the bike path, so she begrudgingly signed up for a Facebook account and found her way to me. I was thrilled to hear that she had adopted a second Greyhound, and that Ferrin and his new housemate were two very happy campers. We laughed at some of my Internet antics, and decided that a play date for the dogs was a must. We remembered old bike rides, dog quirks, forgotten friends. Our old friendship had been rekindled by an unwitting facilitator: Nigel.

Another old friend and I recently had the chance to spend time together. I say old friend, but should say new old friend. In this Internet age, many of us foster long-term relationships that never involve a face to face meeting—consider your long term blogging pals, Facebook friends, Internet group members that you stay in close contact with—despite the fact that you have never met in person. In this case it was an old business relationship that had led to hundreds of calls, a flurry of instant messages lobbed at one another to gripe about work hassles: significant deals closed together under tremendous pressure. Five years of high stress business interactions had drawn us closer, had made friends of strangers, and had pointed out to both of us the upside of technology and its ability to make the world smaller.

Last week we had a chance to seal the deal. A big development at work meant that this old friend would have to fly in to town to spend a day in meetings with me. We both grinned like fools when he stepped in to my office. Five years of hard work, late nights, countless e-mail exchanges and contracts were forgotten as we just stood there beaming, our friendship consummated in a timeless act that could never take place online: a handshake.

When the closing bell rang at work, we ran for the doors. I drove far too quickly, whisking him out of Burlington and into the mountains where we reside. As we entered the house, I paused to observe the moment I had anxiously awaited. My old friend dropped everything, crouched down in the kitchen, and was swallowed up by our unreasonably happy pack of dogs.

He had spent five years watching them grow from afar. He remembered the first Sola blog post. We had both shared many laughs at work as we watched the dogs on a webcam I had set up to babysit them while I was bringing home the bacon. Every time we spoke, he reminded me to kiss the dogs for him—not once, but four times each. For five years. Now, he was swimming in them.

We spent the evening celebrating. The dogs played to the brink of exhaustion. We grabbed a giant flashlight and took a late night tour of the river in front of the house and the surrounding forest. Half of a bottle of Johnny Walker scotch disappeared into my old friend, and there was laughter in abundance. We marveled at our ability to fall into this comfortable place considering that we had never actually met before this day.

The night was too quickly spent. At one in the morning we gave up the ghost and put the cap back on the scotch bottle. My old friend had to fly out the next morning at ten, and I had a number of contracts to button up before the weekend. He spent many minutes saying goodbye to each dog before we departed. We wound our way out of the hills, my car screaming in the night, both of us giddy to be propelled through the darkness by an abundance of horsepower. At one thirty in the morning he fell out of my car and spilled in to the hotel lobby as I laughed hysterically. I departed in a cloud of tire smoke, knowing that he would struggle to sober up in time to make his flight. He did.

I drove home in quiet contemplation, sadness and glee washing over me in equal measure. I could not help but marvel at the power of friendship and its ability to invigorate. The ominous forest surrounding me whizzed by as the speedometer reached for the hundred mark, my iPod spinning a random selection from the *mellow* playlist. The finer details of the commute were lost on me as I considered old friends and all we had shared.

My key turned slowly in the lock at as I returned to the house. It was nearly two in the morning, and I was doing my best not to alarm the dogs. I flipped on the kitchen light and was immediately and enthusiastically greeted by another old friend. It was Nigel.

He is a creature of habit: he lives by routine, and my late night departure had troubled him. He spent the next thirty minutes expressing his relief at my return, his frantic kisses suggesting that it was *not* acceptable to abandon our family members after the clock strikes midnight. He pressed in to me, shaking, hiding his snout under my armpit and giving me a firm push to remind me that old friends stick together in the darkness. I comforted him, snuck him a late treat, and wrapped him in his blanket once he had time to realize that home order had been restored.

I loved him for worrying. I bade him good evening and flipped the last remaining light switch as I made my way up the stairs, fell into bed and lost consciousness, my dreams awash in new memories. One of my oldest and dearest friends slept a floor below me, a sentinel on the sofa keeping watch over our family in the pure, silent blackness of a moonless autumn night.

http://petfinder.com/blog/

Petfinder

Petfinder.com is an online, searchable database of animals who need homes. It is also a directory of more than 13,500 animal shelters and adoption organizations across the U.S., Canada and Mexico. The Petfinder blog features information about pet adoption, care, training, and health as well as suggestions for fun and creative ways to help adoptable pets and to get involved with your local shelter or rescue organization. And of course, no pet adoption blog would be complete without weekly adoption stories.

Favorite Posts:

Shooting Down Common Myths about Pet Adoption
By Jane Harrell on October 2, 2009

We recently ran a post about a *New York Times* columnist who bought a dog even though her young son had urged her to adopt.

The reason? Her husband wanted a Golden Retriever -- or at least a "bigger dog ... who fetched and swam" -- and they didn't think they'd find one in a shelter.

Our blogger wrote that it's a common misconception that there are no purebreds in shelters (in fact, 25% of shelter pets are purebred). One commenter suggested another misplaced belief:

[T]hat somehow a shelter animal (even a purebred rescue) is somehow less healthy or less valuable. ... People feel [that] spending $800 or $1,000 on a purebred dog or cat is a symbol of how high-class they are as individuals.

So we decided to put together a list of common adoption myths, in the hopes that you can gently point friends toward this post when they talk about why they've got their heart set on buying.

Myth #1: I don't know what I'm getting.

There may in fact be more information available about an adoptable pet than one from a breeder or pet store.

Many of the pets posted on Petfinder are in foster care. Foster parents live with their charges 24-7 and can often tell you, in detail, about the pet's personality and habits. If the pet is at a shelter, the staff or volunteers may be able to tell you what he or she is like.

At the very least, you can ask the staff if the pet was an owner surrender (rather than a stray) and, if so, what the former owner said about him or her. Quite often pets are given up because the owner faced financial or housing issues (more on that later). You can also ask about the health and behavioral evaluations the pet has undergone since arriving at the shelter. In contrast, pet store owners rarely have an idea of what a pet will be like in a home.

Myth #2: I can't find what I want at a shelter.

While it's true that adopting a purebred or a young puppy can require more patience than going to a pet store or breeder, it can also lead to a better match for you and your family, for the reasons described above.

If you can't find the pet you're looking for on Petfinder, don't give up. The Humane Society of the United States estimates that 6-8 million cats and dogs enter shelters each year. Some shelters even maintain waiting lists for specific breeds, so don't be afraid to ask! There are also breed-specific rescues for just about every breed, and most of them post their available pets on Petfinder. (Petfinder can even e-mail you when a pet that fits your criteria is posted -- just click "Save this Search" at the top of your search results page.)

Myth #3: I can get a free pet, so why pay an adoption fee?

According to the National Council on Pet Population Study and Policy (via the ASPCA), approximately 65% of pet parents in the U.S. get their pets for free or at low cost, and most pets are obtained from acquaintances or family members. The NCPPSP also reports that pets acquired from friends make up more than 30% of pets surrendered to shelters.

While getting a "free" pet may seem like a bargain at first, you're then responsible for veterinary costs that shelters and rescue groups usually cover, including:

- Spaying/neutering: $150-300
- Distemper vaccination: $20-30 x2
- Rabies vaccination: $15-25
- Heartworm test: $15-35
- Flea/tick treatment: $50-200
- Microchip: $50

Myth #4: I'll be "rescuing" a sick puppy from a pet store.

Pet stores play on our sympathies by keeping pets in small enclosures and in storefronts. But paying the pet store to let you "save" the puppy or kitten gives those stores exactly what they want -- income -- and perpetuates a cruel industry.

Myth #5: Pets are in shelters because they didn't make good pets.

In fact, the main reasons pets are given up include:

- Owners are moving to housing that don't allow pets (7% dogs, 8% cats)
- Allergies (8% cats)

- Owner having personal problems (4% dogs and cats)
- Too many or no room for litter mates (7% dogs, 17% cats)
- Owner can no longer afford the pet (5% dogs, 6% cats)
- Owner no longer has time for the pet (4% dogs)

As you can see, many of the reasons have nothing to do with the pets themselves. Working with shelter staff and volunteers can be a great way to figure out the best match for you and your home.

Myth #6: Shelter pets have too much baggage.

Rescued pets have full histories ... something that can actually be GREAT for adopters. Remember, all pets-- even eight-week old puppies and kittens -- have distinct personalities. Those personalities will either jive with your home and lifestyle or not. Work with rescue group or shelter staff to find the right fit for you.

Ten Reasons Senior Pets Rule
By Jane Harrell on November 1, 2010

November is Adopt-A-Senior-Pet Month! As mom to three "older" cats and one 20-year-old turtle, I consider senior-pet adoption a cause near and dear to my heart.

If you have a friend who's thinking of adopting—or if you're considering adding a new furry family member yourself—read and share this list:

Ten reasons senior pets rule:

1. When senior pets are adopted, they seem to understand that they've been rescued and are all the more thankful for it.

2. A senior pet's personality has already developed, so you'll know if he or she is a good fit for your family.

3. You can teach an old dog (or cat or other pet) new tricks. (I do every day with my own cats!) Senior pets have the attention span and impulse control that makes them easier to train than their youthful counterparts.

4. A senior pet may very well already know basic commands anyway!

5. In particular, senior pets are often already housetrained, or can be more easily housetrained than a young pet with a tiny bladder.

6. A senior pet won't grow any larger, so you'll know exactly how much pet you're getting.

7. Senior pets are often content to just relax in your company, unlike younger pets, who may get into mischief because they're bored.

8. Speaking of relaxing, senior pets make great napping buddies.

9. Senior pets know that chew toys (not shoes) are for chewing and scratching posts (not furniture) are for scratching.

10. Senior pets are some of the hardest to find homes for—so when you adopt a senior pet, you're truly saving a life.

Cognitive Dysfunction Syndrome: What Are the Signs of Dementia in Pets?
By Jane Harrell on April 6, 2011

Aging pets, like people, can suffer mental decline that is not considered a normal part of aging. Recently we wrote about cognitive dysfunction syndrome, or CDS, in senior pets. This week we're looking at its common symptoms.

Recognizing and diagnosing cognitive problems in pets can be tricky. "Many pet owners think their older dog is losing his vision or hearing when in fact the pet is having a hard time recognizing or identifying certain sights or sounds," says Calabash, NC-based veterinarian Ernie Ward.

Is your pet showing signs of CDS? Only your vet can tell you for sure, but it's important that you carefully observe any changes in your pet's behavior. According to the Ohio State University College of Veterinary Medicine, these are the key symptoms to look out for:

- **Disorientation** - Has your pet suddenly "forgotten" how to climb the stairs? Does he get "lost" on walks or walk into corners that he could navigate well before?

- **Interaction changes** - Is your lap cat suddenly aloof, or has your independent dog become clingy?
- **Sleep/wake cycle changes** - Has your pet started pacing at night when he used to be a good sleeper? Does he sleep more during the day than he did before?
- **House soiling** - Is your cat missing the litter box or has your dog stopped letting you know when he needs to go out? Does it seem like he's lost control of his bladder?
- **Activity-level changes** - Does your pet become upset when you leave or seem generally more anxious? Has his appetite decreased? Has he stopped loving his favorite toy, game or treat? Has he stopped grooming himself?

With all changes in your pet's behavior, your vet will want to rule out illness as a cause. "What may be seen as a loss of housetraining—a sign of cognitive dysfunction -- may actually be signs of kidney failure or urinary tract infection," says Dr. Janet Tobiassen Crosby DVM, veterinary medicine columnist for About.com. "These may occur as separate conditions or be concurrent."

Next time: How your vet will diagnose cognitive dysfunction syndrome and what questions you should ask him or her.

Pet Health Care Gazette

Behind the Blog: Lorie Huston, DVM

Kitty Condo: Rhode Island

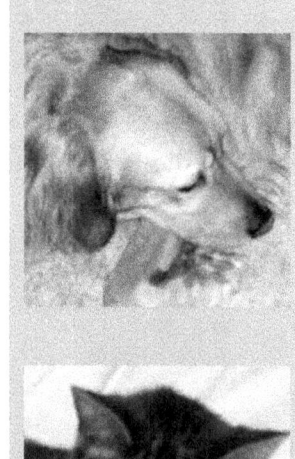

Lorie Huston began writing the Pet Health Care Gazette to empower animal-lovers with the knowledge they need to keep their pets happy and healthy. The blog is based on the following fundamental beliefs:

- Pets enrich our lives. They are cherished members of our families. In a very real sense, they are like our children.
- Pets are loyal companions and friends, providing us with endless hours of comfort and joy, but they rely completely on us to provide for their needs.
- Our pets deserve to feel vibrant and energized from birth to old age.
- Our pets deserve to live long, healthy lives free of pain, discomfort, fear or disease, regardless of their age.

Favorite Posts:

To Vaccinate or *Not* to Vaccinate Your Dog or Cat: Which is Safest?
August 26, 2010

One of the most frequent questions that I am asked in my veterinary practice is, "What vaccines do my kitten (puppy, dog, or cat) need?" Right behind that is, "How often does my pet need to be vaccinated?" Thirdly, and perhaps most importantly, is the question, "Are these vaccines safe for my pet?"

Are vaccines safe for pets?

Let's start by answering the last question first. Both canine and feline vaccinations carry the risk of side effects, just like any other medication. There are very few, if any, medications that come with no risk.

So, the question becomes, why give vaccines to a pet if there is risk involved? The answer to that question is that there is also great benefit in vaccinating pets. In some cases, these vaccines can be life-saving.

A good example of the life-saving aspect of vaccination is in the recent of outbreak of parvovirus that my hospital and others in the area have been seeing within the last few weeks. In my hospital, we have seen literally dozens of puppies infected with parvovirus. Unfortunately, not all of these puppies have survived the infection.

What do all of these puppies have in common? None of them, not a single one that I have seen, have been adequately vaccinated against this disease. For most if not all of these puppies, the parvovirus vaccination would have prevented the infection and kept them healthy.

Parvovirus vaccinations for puppies, a true life example

One really unfortunate case was a five-month-old puppy who was obtained from a breeder. The breeder informed the puppy's new owner that the puppy should not receive any vaccines prior to six months of age because it would be unsafe for the puppy. Unfortunately, the new owner believed the breeder was providing accurate information when, in fact, the information was incorrect. Because of the misinformation provided by an ill-informed layperson together with the innocent lack of knowledge possessed by a well-meaning pet owner, the puppy did not live to be six months of age. She expired a few days ago of a disease that could easily have been prevented by proper vaccination.

The case against vaccination for dogs and cats

There are a number of people who advocate not vaccinating dogs and cats. Their fears do carry some weight. Vaccinations have been implicated in contributing to or even causing some types of cancer. Vaccines are also suspected to cause disorders of immune function as well as other medical issues.

I do not dispute these possibilities nor do I discount their importance. However, I cannot look past the fact that vaccines can protect dogs and cats (and particularly puppies and kittens) from deadly diseases. In my opinion, if a dog or cat dies of a preventable disease such as canine parvovirus or feline distemper because of a lack of proper vaccination, it really makes very little difference what types of problem that vaccine could potentially cause many years from the vaccination date.

What vaccinations are necessary for a dog or cat? Puppy or kitten?

The answer to that question depends on the lifestyle and individual risks encountered by that particular pet. Vaccine schedules and protocols are not a one-size-fits-all proposal. A pet owner is best advised to discuss with his or her veterinarian which vaccinations are necessary for each individual pet.

How often should vaccines be administered?

Again, the answer depends on the individual pet and the type of vaccine being used. This is also a matter that a pet owner should discuss with his or her veterinarian. Some vaccines need to be given every three years; others need to be repeated yearly. Your veterinarian can determine, with your help, which vaccines your pet needs (and which he does not need) and develop a logical vaccination schedule that can help keep your pet healthy and happy.

In the coming weeks, we'll be discussing in more depth the individual canine and feline vaccines that are available. So stay tuned. But remember that this material is meant for education purposes only and your best source of information about your pet is your own veterinarian.

Cats are Not Small Dogs
March 28, 2011

Photo Courtesy of elsie esq/Flickr.com

Those of you who own and love cats probably already know that cats are not small dogs. However, you might be surprised how many people treat them as though they are.

Cats and dogs are actually quite different from one another in many ways. Physiologically, anatomically, behaviorally and nutritionally, there are major differences between dogs and cats.

Cats have special nutritional needs

Cats have special nutritional needs that differ from those of dogs. Feeding a cat a diet meant for a dog can be detrimental for your cat. Always feed your cat a diet that is formulated to be balanced and complete for a cat's nutritional needs.

Cats and medicines

Cats are sensitive to many medications that dogs can take quite safely. This is true of many different types of medications but it is especially true of flea and tick medications. Never treat your cat with a flea or tick product that is not labeled specifically for cats. If the label does not say the product is safe for cats, it likely is not.

Many over-the-counter drugs are not safe for cats. These include medicines like Tylenol and aspirin (though these are not entirely safe for dogs, either!).

In general, before you treat your cat with any medication that is not prescribed specifically for your cat and/or not labeled for cats, you should consult a veterinarian for advice.

Feline behavior

Behaviorally, cats are much different than dogs. This likely does not come as a shock to most cat owners. However, many cat owners fail to realize how stress can affect their cat and what their cat may find stressful. Though dogs may be affected by stress as well, I believe that cats (arguably) are bothered by it to a greater degree.

What can happen to a cat that is experiencing stress? They are prone to developing numerous physical illnesses as a result. Cystitis in cats is often related to stress and many veterinarians believe that bladder problems are only the tip of the iceberg. Gastrointestinal problems and respiratory disease can also occur in cats kept under stressful conditions.

Sebastian the Sensitive Soul

Sebastian the Sensitive Soul is a place where Sebastian can blog about whatever is on his mind. He loves to talk about pets waiting for their forever homes at Wayside Waifs. He also likes to blog about things happening in his life, be it a trip to the vet, a visit from his Grandma and Grandpa, or maybe the birds and squirrels in the tree outside the bedroom window. He truly is a sensitive kitty.

He keeps a running slideshow of photos of adoptable pets on the sidebar, as well as badges from organizations he supports. Sebastian will occasionally do reviews for products we really like, too.

Behind the Blog: Amy Palmer

Inspired By: Sebastian (American shorthair cat)

Kitty Condo: Kansas

Favorite Posts:

Blankets for Kitties
January 2, 2011

Recently when Mom was volunteering at Wayside Waifs, another volunteer brought in some fleece blankies she bought at a STEAL! Her idea was to make some no-sew blankets—you know, the kind that are tied all along the edges. They were going to be especially for the kitties waiting for adoption. Mom thought this was a great idea and so did a couple other volunteers. They got right to work in the sun room at Wayside.

They wanted the blankies to be *purr*fectly kitty-sized, so they took each blanket and cut it into four blankets. Then they took the different patterns and put them together so they would look nice with a solid color on one side and stripes on the other.

They giggled and laughed the whole time they were making the kitty blankies. None of them knew what they were doing, but boy, did they have a good time! Even one of the available cats helped them.

This is Simba holding down some material for Lindsay. He checked out all the blankets and made sure they were comfy enough for the kitties.

It took a long time, but soon they had four blankets done and they all gave the blanket they made to a special kitty. Simba got the one he helped Lindsay with. Mom gave hers to Anderson.

Aren't volunteers the best? They all love the kitties very much and make sure they have something special, something that is just theirs, while they stay at Wayside Waifs. In fact, Anderson is going to get to take his blankie home with him when he finds his forever home—Mom said so!

Grandma and Grandpa's Visit
October 26, 2010

My Grandma and Grandpa came to stay with us last weekend. It was the second time they were here since I came to live with Mom. It was so much fun! Grandma brought me a bag of treats and let me sit on her lap.

Grandpa didn't want me to sit on his lap, but I tried a few times anyway. He always said no. That's okay. Some people just prefer to look at me, I guess.

Grandma talked to me a lot while she was here. I like to talk often, and when I did, she would have a conversation with me. She even let me go into the bathroom with her when she got ready for bed at night.

It was fun having my grandparents visit. I hope other *anipals* get visits like this, too. It made me feel like a very special kitty.

Blog the Change for Animals: Chain of Hope
January 15, 2011

For today's Blog the Change for Animals, started by the great folks over at Be the Change for Animals, I was thinking about posting about Wayside Waifs. Those of you who frequently read my blog know how important Wayside has been in my life. That's where I met Mom and where she volunteers. They have the best people over there. You can even read what my pal Ryker's mom has to say about them in her Blog the Change post today. Since I talk about Wayside all the time, I decided to post about a different local group.

There is a grassroots organization in Kansas City, MO called Chain of Hope. It was started by Kate Quigley in 2010 as a way to reach dogs in the inner city that are chained; without shelter, food or water; neglected or homeless. She and her volunteers will drive around until they find a dog who needs their help. They provide lighter tie-outs for dogs on heavy tow chains. They give doghouses with fresh hay to dogs living in mud with no protection from the elements. They feed and water dogs whose owners aren't able to care for them.

They don't just care for the dogs, though. They also provide education. They knock on doors and talk to the dog owners. If the owners agree, they take the dogs to be spayed or neutered. Sometimes, the owner gives up the dog altogether, and Chain of Hope fosters it until he or she finds his or her forever home.

Dealing with these situations is not always easy. If a dog is completely neglected and the owner can't be reached, Chain of Hope calls Animal Control and reports the situation. At times, it is too late for the dogs that Chain of Hope encounters. They might find them near death, and the only way to help is to get the dog to a vet, so it can be humanely euthanized rather than made to suffer any longer.

Chain of Hope regularly holds fundraising efforts to help sustain the organization. Mom went to one not long ago at a local bar. Many people came and brought food, treats and most importantly, cash. She met Ms. Quigley there and was amazed at what this one woman has accomplished. Mom sees her as a hero, somebody to strive to be like. Ms. Quigley is an inspiration and a model for what all humans can do to help animals. Like her quote on the front page of their website says, **"...if we can change the life of even one dog, it matters."**

You can learn more about Chain of Hope and "like" their Facebook page. You can also read their blog. My favorite story was a recent one about Jackson, whom they helped to reunite with his owner. If you are in the KC area, I hope you will support Chain of Hope. Get to know them, spread the word, donate and maybe even volunteer.

And for my kitty friends—don't worry. Ms. Quigley feeds the felines she comes across, too!

http://speakingforspot.com/blog/

Speaking for Spot

Behind the Blog: Dr. Nancy Kay, DVM

Inspired By: Quinn (mixed-breed dog)

Doghouse: California

Speaking for Spot was a labor of love for Dr. Nancy Kay, fueled by her passion to teach people how to be effective medical advocates for their four-legged best friends. Gone are the days of simply following doc's orders—today's dog lovers are confronted with health-care decision-making on many levels.

Dr. Nancy Kay wanted to become a veterinarian for just about as long as she can remember. Her veterinary degree is from Cornell College of Veterinary Medicine, and she completed her residency training in small animal internal medicine at the University of California—Davis Veterinary School.

Dr. Kay is a board certified specialist in the American College of Veterinary Internal Medicine and published in several professional journals and textbooks. She lectures professionally to regional and national audiences, and one of her favorite lecture topics is communication between veterinarians and their clients. Since the release of her book, *Speaking for Spot: Be the Advocate Your Dog Needs to Live a Happy, Healthy, Longer Life,* Dr. Kay has lectured extensively and written numerous magazine articles on the topic of medical advocacy. She was a featured guest on the popular National Public Radio show, *Fresh Air with Terry Gross.*

Dr. Kay is a staff internist at VCA Animal Care Center, a 24-hour emergency/specialty care center in Rohnert Park, California. As a way of providing emotional support for people with sick four-legged family members, Dr. Kay founded and helps facilitate the VCA Animal Care Center Client Support Group. She also facilitates client communication rounds for VCA Animal Care Center employees.

Dr. Kay was selected by the American Animal Hospital Association to receive the 2009 Hill's Animal Welfare and Humane Ethics Award. This award is given annually to a veterinarian or non-veterinarian who has advanced animal welfare through extraordinary service or by furthering humane principles, education and understanding. The Dog Writers Association of America selected Dr. Kay for two awards. The first was the 2009 Eukanuba Canine Health Award recognizing Speaking for Spot as the publication that best promotes the health and well being of dogs. The second award was for the Best Blog of 2009 (www.speakingforspot.com/blog). Dr. Kay was also the recipient of the 2011 "Leo K. Bustad Companion Animal Veterinarian of the Year" award, which is presented annually to a veterinarian whose work promotes and exemplifies the human-animal bond.

Dr. Kay's personal life revolves around her husband (also a veterinarian), her three children (none of whom aspire to be veterinarians) and their menagerie of four-legged family members. When she's not writing, she spends her spare moments in the garden or riding along the beach atop her favorite horse. Dr. Kay and her family reside in Northern California.

Victims Come in All Sizes
February 20, 2009

As I was hanging out in the midst of our busy hospital treatment room during emergency hours a few nights ago, I was impressed at how much was going on all at once. On one treatment table was a pregnant Chihuahua experiencing difficulty passing her pups. On another table was a 13-year-old dog in a state of shock after trauma inflicted by other dogs in the neighborhood. An anesthetized kitty with a urinary tract blockage was being tended to on a third table. Things got even busier when a receptionist entered the treatment room with two stray Rottweilers in tow. The woman who dropped them off said she found them in a local shopping center parking lot. Both Rotties were gorgeous with wonderfully sweet dispositions. Their little stub-tailed hind ends wiggled frantically in response to our attention. Additionally, it was apparent that both dogs were profoundly pregnant.

We hoped these two girls just happened to have busted out of their yard—perhaps a gate had been left open. We envisioned an anxious family frantic to find their pregnant dogs. Our optimism quickly dissipated as we discovered no collars, no identification microchips and no one searching to reclaim their lost dogs, in spite of our efforts to let every local shelter, pound and veterinary hospital know about our new charges. Looking back, it seemed a bit suspicious that the woman who dropped them off happened to have a crate in the back of her truck big enough to hold two large dogs.

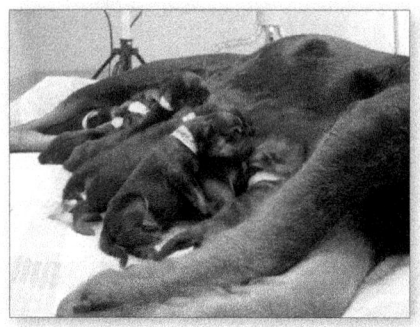

We turned one of our visiting rooms into a whelping pen and over the course of three hours, our two strays morphed into 12, as one of the dogs delivered 10 beautiful, healthy pups. Some of them looked like "mom;" others revealed that "dad" was something other than a Rottweiler. Mama was a natural—licking and cleaning—doing everything just right, including letting complete strangers cut umbilical cords, inspect puppies, change bedding and take her out for potty breaks while telling her what a perfect princess she was. Thus far, mama number two had not yet whelped.

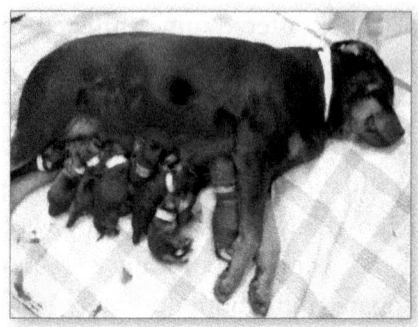

I found myself longing to know the names of these two dogs (thinking they would enjoy hearing them) and wondering if they were missing their favorite humans. Clearly, both had been well socialized and cared for. They had sleek, shiny haircoats and substantial body weights. And why were they given up? Were all of these dogs simply victims of tough economic times? Perhaps the prospects of finding homes for so many non-purebred pups was daunting. The good news was that these mothers found their way to a "birthing center," where they and their pups would be well cared for.

While we awaited the arrival of litter number two, plans were in the works to place moms and pups with one or two Rottweiler rescue organizations. The big-hearted people who run such rescue organizations (some are breed-specific, others are not) are intent on making sure that needy dogs get second chances.

Mia, Candy and 15 Puppies
March 8, 2009

It has now been two weeks since two pregnant Rottweilers were abandoned at my hospital. My blog post about these two girls generated so much interest about their welfare, I feel the need to provide an update.

Within days of having their lives turned upside down, one of the Rottweilers (now named Mia) gave birth to 10 plump, vigorous, hungry puppies: six girls and four boys. She and her pups are receiving foster care and living the good life with Jill (one of our hospital receptionists) and her family. Jill tells me that this has been an incredible and wonderful experience for her family. They have fallen in love with Mia (they may have trouble letting her go), and watching the puppies change day by day has been extraordinary. Mia is the "model mom," nurturing her pups and welcoming the companionship of her new human family. The pups have just opened their eyes and are quickly developing different personalities. Some are calm and unobtrusive while others have become pushy, persistently demanding their mama's attention and pushing others out of the way to get it. The pups are named (at least temporarily) Abby, Bandit, Charli, Delilah, Ember, Freda, Giovani, Hans, Ivan and Juno. A few look like Rottweilers; the others clearly have mixed-breed markings. To date, six of Mia's pups are spoken for.

Candy and her puppies have found a safe haven with Rottweiler maven, Linda. Like so many others who tirelessly invest their time and money into dog rescue work, Linda opens her home and heart to Rottweilers (or Rottweiler mixed-breeds), who have experienced misfortune. Linda reports that, in the course of adapting to so many changes, Candy's somewhat timid demeanor is giving way to a more animated, tail-wagging personality. Like Mia, Candy is also a wonderful mother. To date, none of her pups are spoken for. There are three boys and two girls.

I continue to ponder what life must have been like for Mia and Candy before I met them and why the person who cared for them felt the need to make such a drastic life-changing decision. What I do know is that, from here on out, life is bound to be wonderful for these two gorgeous mothers and their 15 babies.

Magic!
March 17, 2009

Magic was an incredibly smart and affectionate Rottweiler-mix, lovingly cared for by Matt, Shannon and their two children. Her final years were a challenge because of diabetes and blindness. When the quality of Magic's life dramatically diminished and there was no hope for improvement, Matt and Shannon opted for euthanasia. Magic passed away peacefully at my hospital while lying on her favorite blue-and-white checkered blanket, surrounded by her doting human family members.

That was just a few months ago. When I've spoken with Matt and Shannon since, it became clear that Magic's absence has created a huge void. They and their children are all experiencing and working through their grief a little bit differently. Not surprisingly, they've had some debates about when to consider adopting another dog. The kids are clearly ready. Matt and Shannon haven't been so sure, that is, until they received my email about two abandoned Rottweiler mamas and their 15 mixed-breed puppies. The photos that accompanied my description of the dogs were utterly compelling to them. Not only did the appearance of the mother remind them of their Magic, the blanket she and her pups were lying on happened to be the exact same blue-and-white checkered blanket they'd left at my hospital with their beloved girl (keep in mind, we have literally hundreds of blankets to choose from in our hospital)!

Needless to say, a quick family conference determined that a puppy visit was in order. Now Matt, Shannon and their kids have only a few more weeks to wait before Charlie, a plump little female with German Shepherd-type markings, becomes part of their family. What a lucky puppy!

Some refer to such interesting life events as synchronicity. Deepak Chopra would likely refer to this story as a "divine coincidence." I prefer to think of it as Magic!

A Rottweiler Reunion
March 27, 2010

If you've been following my blog for some time, you may remember a series of stories I posted about two pregnant Rottweilers that were abandoned at my veterinary hospital. In fact, these girls were so darned pregnant that, within 24 hours, one of them, now named Mia, delivered 10 healthy, happy puppies. Mia and her little sausages were fostered by Jill, a member of the amazing team of receptionists at my hospital. Jill ended up keeping the runt of the litter, now known as Dodger, and she managed to find wonderful homes for Mia and the other nine pups. Candy, the other mama, found her way to Linda, a Rottweiler maven who works tirelessly doing Rottie rescue work. Candy delivered five pups while in Linda's care. Mama and all five pups were placed in caring homes.

Jill has managed to keep tabs on Mia and all but one her puppies. As the adoptive families report, they are all matches made in heaven! At their recent one-year birthday reunion (held at a local dog park), the puppies were all playing while their humans were sporting grins from ear to ear! Although there were 30 or so dogs at the park that day, the siblings seemed to hang out preferentially with one another. Have a look at the "before" and "after" photos. In the adult photos, there are clearly two distinct facial appearances. (Perhaps two different dads were involved in the creation of this litter!) Charlie, Bandit, and Giovani have kept their original names. Abby, Bandit, Delilah, Ember, Freda, Hans, Ivan, and Juno have become Maggie, Dee Dee, Dodger, Ava, Trixie, Bruno, and Sadie.

Those little sausages have all turned into massive dogs with weights varying from 80 to 110 pounds. And guess who the 110 pounder is? None other than Dodger, the original runt of the litter!

I hope this blog makes you smile and reminds you to support your local animal rescue organizations.

*Photos courtesy of Matt Stevens

http://thisonewildlife.com/

This One Wild Life

ThisOneWildLife.com celebrates the everyday joy we humans experience when interacting with animals, whether domestic or wild, while advocating for animal health and welfare in the rescue and pet world as well as the natural environment we share.

Celebrate rescue animals!

Let fly a rousing bout of laughter as we share the hilarious antics of our beloved rescue animals: Shamus, the Newf; Emmett, a zany hound-mix; Jackson and Jed, twin tabbies born three weeks apart to the same mother from different fathers (crazy, indeed); Frankie Sinatra and Ella "Yella Bird" Fitzgerald, our crooning cockatiels; and a non-speaking parakeet named Wordsworth.

Celebrate wildlife!

Enjoy exciting and informative wildlife adventures at our log cabin in Upstate New York and along our travels from Alaska to California, New Jersey, Ghana, the Bahamas and Mexico, with more destinations to come.

Behind the Blog:
Kim Clune

Inspired By:
Shamus (Newfoundland), Emmett (hound-mix), Jackson & Jed (orange tabbies)

Doghouse:
New York

The people behind the blog

This One Wild Life is brought to you by animal lover, author, photographer and videographer, Kim Clune, with the help of her husband, Tim Clune, a man dedicated to animal rescue for more than 20 years. With an ever-growing cast of characters, we can assure you – there is never a dull moment in what we call This One Wild Life.

Both Dogs: Lost ... and Found
February 12, 2011

As the dogs bask quietly in the sun, it's difficult to imagine how we survived the past two days. That we are together again is testament to a happy ending, but its fruition wasn't always expected...

The snow stair

The trouble started with several brutal storms while we vacationed in Mexico last week. Our house sitter called to say that, after 20 inches of snow, sleet and freezing rain, Shamus, our Newf, leveraged this new mantel to jump the fence. Thankfully, true to Newf form, Shamus appreciates companionship more than freedom. He came back immediately. We were lucky.

When our sitter shoveled snow from the point of exit, the problem appeared to be solved – until it wasn't. Shamus found another weight-bearing point. The only solution, until we came home, was sentencing Shamus to doggy jail at the maximum security kennel – along with Emmett, who would surely learn this new trick too.

The "No!" stare

Upon our return to more freezing rain, we waited impatiently for the 40 degrees of melt promised by the weather man. I supervised the dogs' outings while Tim left town for several days. On Wednesday, Shamus oh-so-obviously made calculations to jump. I wagged my finger and said "No, no, no!" calling both dogs back for treats. This worked so well that, in subsequent recalls, Shamus came back with expectations before doing his business. Overkill, obviously. But it kept him contained.

Getting a jump on things

Tim promised to clear the fence of snow when he returned, but I wanted to do my part too. I chipped, beat and hefted layers of snow infused with ice as strong as steel reinforcements, creating an inside mote 2-½ feet deep and spanning four post lengths. It felt like an enormous feat. I have the back injury to prove it. And it wasn't nearly enough. Our dog yard spans a half acre.

Taking the boys out after dinner that night, Shamus showed interest in a high drift. I moved down the hill yelling "Don't do it! No!" as he crouched his back legs to spring. He took the leap as my feet flew forward, my head hit the ground and my back locked in a twinge. Before I could get up, Emmett whined for his departed pack-mate and climbed the fence to follow Shamus.

The 20-hour search begins

The temperature was 14 degrees. It was dark. I called the neighbors and all kept their eyes peeled. Audra, my closest neighbor, spread the word and joined my search. Tim left NYC a day early and was home by midnight. While I drove circles around the mountain, he geared up and snowshoed through the woods. For all my boys, Tim included, I feared the worst: injuries, hypothermia, frostbite, a deadly run-in with our resident coyotes.

At 3 a.m., Tim and I settled in to regroup. There was no sleep. Having opened the yard gates and dog door earlier hoping for a return, we listened for any sign. By 6 a.m., the sky turned from pitch black to a hint of dark gray. Tim and I geared up with snowshoes and headed back into the woods together.

Tracking creatures great and small

Emmett had run in spirals trotting gingerly beside turkey tracks until they were crossed by deer tracks, spinning around again after rabbit tracks. Most prints were three-to-six inches deep and they crossed each other, forcing us to look deep into the holes to identify their source. I lost Emmett's trail countless times and picked it up again later only to end where I began.

Tim followed Shamus' tracks, which eventually traveled in a straight line. At times, there were body imprints where Shamus crashed several feet into the deep snow. Tim's snowshoes sank too, at times, and his knees – in need of surgery – ached as he lifted the shoes out for each next step. My back screamed. Pouring sweat, our fingers and toes turned to ice. Each of us, when asking the other how we felt, said we were fine compared to what the dogs must be feeling. We kept moving forward. It was all we could do.

Organizing the search party

Friends and family: By 8 a.m., I returned to greet the search party assembled by Tim: Dawn from Creekside Kennel and our friends Lori and Mike. Mike stayed at the house in case our boys returned in need of medical care. Dawn and Lori drove the streets. Lori picked Tim up along the way.

Local animal services: Leaving our number with animal control, the man seemed scattered and offered little comfort. Menands Shelter refuses lost dog calls. And Nassau Veterinary Clinic finally offered a ray of sunlight. Christina, at reception, alerted the whole clinic. Debbie, a vet tech, said to call the local highway departments. Every client who walked in the door was made aware— all day long.

Help in unexpected places: Fred and Bob at the Nassau Highway Department not only kept an eye out, but they sent trucks and hiked along the power lines tracking what appears to have been a coyote. Fred even called us that afternoon for updates and friended me on Facebook for news. The Schodack Highway Department spread the word through supervisors and staff.

I dropped off flyers and spoke with people at post offices, gas stations and convenience stores. We spoke with Andy, our mailman, who spread the word to the FedEx and UPS guys. Fliers went to every neighbor's house, Bill at the transfer station and to the propane delivery man.

Coming together: The energy of the entire town and the support of our family and friends gave Tim and me the energy needed to push through our exhaustion and past heads full of frightening, negative thoughts.

A man with a map and a plan

Tim found tracks near a dilapidated trailer home and snowshoed in to learn what direction the dogs were headed. They had been gone 18 hours at this point. We now know they had traveled about six straight miles plus countless zig-zags. It was two hours before sunset and temps were dropping to 10 degrees. The good news? Shamus and Emmett were traveling together.

With a lead on their trail, Tim entered the opposite side of the woods hoping to meet them head on. I drove to the trailer to wait. There was no guarantee the dogs were still here, but it was worth looking.

After hiking a mile in, Tim called asking me to lay on the horn so he could follow the sound out. I honked. He heard nothing. A few minutes later, I honked again. He still heard nothing. He decided to keep hiking while I widened the search around the mountain.

Before we hung up, I told Tim about a snow boulder that rolled off the plow stack in front of my car. It wasn't there the first two times I drove by, yet it now faced me – featuring a giant, yellow pee stain. I laughed and said, "Maybe it's a sign!" One could only hope. We hung up and I drove off.

I've got them!

Moments later, Tim called and said, "I've got them."

What? But where is he? After several dropped cell connections, I went back to his car so we could meet up and called Nassau Vet to say we'd bring both dogs soon. Tim came out of the woods and I ran out of the car to help him, tears flowing. The dogs pulled him toward me with exuberance and, together, Tim and I put them in the car.

I looked at Tim, astonished. They looked incredible. "Are they okay?"

He shrugged with doubt. "Their pads are bleeding. They're shaking. They flung themselves in the snow to rest several times while I walked them out."

I looked in the back seat. My boys were now slumped trembling against one another. Their heads merged with the car seat. The skin hung loose from their faces, deflated. The energetic trot toward me was fleeting.

Tim recalled how he yelled their names and heard Shamus bark. As he moved closer in his hat, sunglasses, coat, gloves and snowshoes, they both barked defensively. When he took off his hat, glasses and gloves, Shamus came post-holing through the snow, collapsing into Tim's legs. Emmett bounded after, plowing his body into Shamus for warmth. Tim said Emmett's eyes expressed a grateful sense of relief at being rescued. The dogs were not enjoying their adventure. They were very confused, scared and lost.

The impossible vet exam

Emmett lay wilted, shivering in the sun on the waiting room floor. He looked 60 pounds worth of small wrapped in Tim's big, red parka. A ravenous Shamus briefly begged for treats from the counter, then greeted newcomers with a weak but wagging tail. We entered the exam room separately, each boy getting a thorough once over.

I don't know how or why, but there was no hypothermia. Nothing appeared broken. There was no frostbite. We were told Shamus looked like he enjoyed his adventure and Emmett just seemed exhausted. With pain meds to ease the aches of their vigorous hike, we were to feed and water them as usual and let them rest. It was a miracle.

Then, at check-out, Debbie called to say she had taken down the LOST flier at the post office. Tim took down the one at Stewart's. How very satisfying.

The aftermath

We brought water bowls to our exhausted dogs in their beds, made rounds of thank-you calls, and our reunited pack fell asleep shortly after dinner. We slept straight on 'til morning.

The dogs were traumatized the next day, refusing to go outside, even after so many hours of sleep. We coaxed them out after breakfast and they limped painfully through the yard. Each stuck close to his or her humans until they relieved themselves in grand quantities and returned to the house. When the dogs were safely inside, all my emotions broke free.

Sleeping for hours on my watch and as Tim came home from work to shovel, Shamus didn't climb the stairs to sleep with us. Things still weren't right. Last night, Shamus stopped bearing weight on his left, front paw. We iced it, offered pain meds. Seeing our boy in pain is torturous. We hunkered down on the floor with him and moved to bed only after Shamus was more comfortable. Would this nightmare ever end?

We brought Shamus back to Nassau Vet this morning. X-rays showed no breaks. Tendinitis is likely the culprit. A questionable flap of skin could be a tiny bit of frostbite, or the housing for a thorn. We have new pain meds, a wrap and antibiotics. The improvement since has been tremendous. My heart may finally stop breaking.

On the way home once more, I had the chance to take down another flier. I now knew the relief Tim and Debbie felt removing the others. There is nothing better than saying, "We found them!"

Today we spent hours clearing the rest of the snow by hand, me chipping away at ice, Tim shoveling it away, each of us making the yard safe once more. The dogs came out with confidence today. I think we may have crossed to the other side of this.

It's time to finally move on...

Whistler: The Barred Owl
March 8, 2011

Massive, magical, mythical wings beat silently through crisp winter air. I feel the atmosphere shift, even from within the house. Suddenly, a blurred flurry of motion. My eyes see what I had only sensed. A barred owl flaps past my window then glides upward with graceful lift, landing softly in our dormant maple. Downy feathers fluff against the brisk chill, shrouding a pair of massive feet. The hard stare of two big, black eyes softens as they close, slowly. Mine are wide with wonder, consuming the majesty of this magnificent being napping before me.

Three times in a week, the owl returns, cozying up to our feeders for several hours before sunset. The head slowly turns. Facial feathers hone in, gathering sounds of scrambling squirrels and curious cardinals. Interest takes hold but the mood is fleeting, set adrift like a feather on a gentle breeze as sleep settles in.

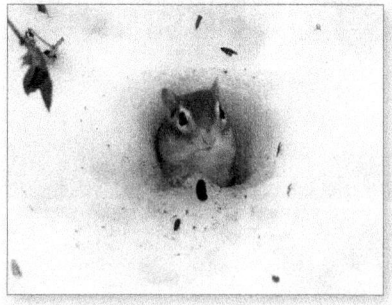

With each visit, the owl lingers longer, closer, allowing me to open the window, to speak, to photograph. My unyielding attention is ignored but for my disruption of dinner, when I startle a curious chipmunk back into his snow bank—on purpose.

http://thoughtsfurpaws.com

Thoughts Fur Paws

Behind the Blog:
Jaime Lynn Smith

In Memory of:
Theodore (domestic shorthair cat)

Kitty Condo:
Ohio

Jaime Lynn Smith refers to herself as a pet fanatic or "Animaniac," like the old cartoon. She loves to write both her Thoughts Fur Paws blog and blogs at The Daily Cat and The Dog Daily, sharing personal stories, educating others, advocating for pets and animals of all types, sizes, and kinds, learning from others and making friends through comment discussions. Smith writes most frequently about animal welfare causes, animal welfare legislation, the politics of "pets" (ex. recent pet causes, the puppy mill industry, product reviews, pet charity, and rescue/shelters), and finally about cats and dogs: breeds, behaviors, nutrition, health, funny stories, pet loss and more. She is also an original poet and professional copywriter, who prides herself on loving, learning and giving. Thoughts Fur Paws is also nationally famous for photo contests and great prizes.

Smith's favorite quote comes from the celebrated Dr. Theodore Seuss: *"Say what you mean and mean what you say because those who matter don't mind, and those who mind don't matter."*

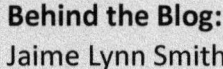

Favorite Posts:

Rescue Dog's Poem: Do I Go Home Today?
March 11, 2011

My family brought me home, cradled in their arms,
They cuddled me and smiled at me and said I was full of charm.
They played with me and laughed with me,
They showered me with toys,
I sure do love my family,
Especially the girls and boys.
The children loved to feed me,
They gave me special treats.
They even let me sleep with them, all snuggled in the sheets.
I used to go for walks, often several times a day,
They even fought to hold the leash, I'm
very proud to say.
They used to laugh and praise me when
I played with that old shoe,
But I didn't know the difference between
the old ones and the new.
The kids and I would grab a rag,
For hours we would tug,
So I thought I did the right thing when I chewed the bathroom rug.
They said that I was out of control and
would have to live outside,
This I didn't understand although I've
tried and tried.
The walks stopped one by one, they said
they hadn't time.
I wish that I could change things.
I wish I knew my crime.
My life became so lonely in the backyard
on a chain,
I barked and barked all day long to keep
from going insane.

So they brought me to the shelter but
were embarrassed to say why,
They said I caused an allergy and then
kissed me goodbye.
If I'd only had some classes as a little pup,
I wouldn't have been so hard to handle
when I was all grown up.
"You only have one day left," I heard the
worker say,
Does this mean a second chance for me,
Do I go home today?

An Abandoned Dog's Rainbow Bridge Story
July 16, 2009

It is said that when animals die they don't go to heaven, they go to the Rainbow Bridge where they wait for their owners. The area around the Rainbow Bridge is sunny, warm but not too warm. Flowers, grass and all the animals have been restored to a youthful healthy state.

On one particular day it was unlike most days at Rainbow Bridge. This day dawned cold and gray, damp as a swamp and as dismal as could be imagined. All of the recent arrivals had no idea what to think. They had never experienced a day like this before.

But the animals who had been waiting for their beloved people knew exactly what was going on and started to gather at the pathway leading to The Bridge to watch.

It wasn't long before an elderly dog came into view, head hung low and tail dragging. The other animals, the ones who had been there for a while, knew what his story was right away, for they had seen this happen far too often.

He approached slowly, obviously in great emotional pain, but with no sign of injury or illness. Unlike all of the other animals waiting at The Bridge, this animal had not been restored to youth and made healthy and vigorous again! As he walked toward The Bridge, he watched all of the other animals watching him. He knew he was out of place here and the sooner he could cross over, the happier he would be.

But, alas, as he approached The Bridge, his way was barred by the appearance of an Angel who apologized, but told him that he would not be able to pass. Only those animals who were with their people could pass over Rainbow Bridge.

With no place else to turn to, the elderly animal turned towards the fields before The Bridge and saw a group of other animals like himself, also elderly. They weren't playing, but rather simply lying on the green grass, forlornly staring out at the pathway leading to The Bridge. And so, he took his place among them, watching the pathway and waiting.

One of the newest arrivals at The Bridge didn't understand what he had just witnessed and asked one of the animals that had been there for a while to explain it to him.

"You see, that poor animal was abandoned by his owners. He was turned into a shelter just as you see him now, an older animal with his fur graying and his eyes clouding. He never made it out of the shelter and passed on. Because he had no family to give his love to, he has no one to escort him across The Bridge."

The first animal thought about this for a minute and then asked, "So what will happen now?"

As he was about to receive his answer, the clouds suddenly parted and the gloom lifted.

Approaching The Bridge could be seen a single person and among the older animals, a whole group was suddenly bathed in a golden light and they were all young and healthy again, just as they were in the prime of life.

"Watch, and see," said the second animal.

A second group of animals from those waiting came to the pathway and bowed low as the person neared. At each bowed head, the person offered a pat on the head or a scratch behind the ears. The newly restored animals fell into line and followed him towards The Bridge.

They all crossed The Bridge together.

"What happened?"

"That was a rescuer. The animals you saw bowing in respect were those who found new homes because of his work. They will cross when their new families arrive. Those you saw restored were those who never found homes. When a rescuer arrives, he or she is allowed to perform one, final act of rescue. They are allowed to escort those poor animals that they couldn't place on earth, across The Rainbow Bridge."

"I think I like rescuers," said the first animal.

"So does GOD," was the reply.

Two Little Cavaliers

Behind the Blog:
Felissa Elfenbein

Two Little Cavaliers was founded in February of 2010 by 30-year-old Felissa Elfenbein to share information about pet health and fun, military dogs, dog rescue, and great pet products. The blog features many giveaways and informative articles.

Inspired By:
Davinia and Indiana (Cavalier King Charles Spaniels)

Doghouse:
Florida

Davina is the older of the two little Cavaliers who inspire the blog, having recently turned seven. She was very small at birth and has required lots of love and attention. Indiana is a six-year-old "tomboy diva dog." Both dogs came from a responsible breeder in rural Germany.

Favorite Posts:

US Military Family Doesn't Want to Leave Pets Behind!
March 16, 2011

I saw a link to a note on Facebook for a desperate plea from a military family being evacuated from Japan today. They are being told they cannot take their pets with them. Do you have any contacts that could help them get their pets out or ensure their safety until they can be put on a plane to join their family?

Mariaelena Rodriguez Geoffray and Bella

Urgent!

A Tehachapi, California, family on active military duty in Japan needs help evacuating their pets along with the family. Here is the message that was received from the family. You can feel the desperation this family is feeling as moment by moment their choices for bringing their pets back to the U.S. deteriorate.

"There will be nobody to fly my animals if I'm gone by tomorrow. Anyway, I have an appointment for the animals to get their health certs at 1:30 my time, and I'll be searching for any flight that can take animals for tomorrow. I don't leave until 6:30 pm, so I have time to spare at the airport. I can't believe this is really happening. The military flights won't fly animals unless I'm on PCS orders. I'm not; we've lived here too long now." *Does anyone have military or government connection that would help?* Our military families in Japan need our support. They should not have to leave their pets behind in an evacuation!

More from the military family: "[..] this is breaking my heart! It's only me and my kids. My husband isn't even here to help out. The animals know something is going on. I'm quickly running out of options.

"I have no idea how to get in contact with those [organizations]. I could just hang out at the airport and hope for the best?

"I'm flying Singapore Air. They do not fly animals at all. They gave me the number to PetMovers. Unbelievable! I'm at Yokota Ab. I will be at Narita Airport tomorrow, 18 March. I just emailed Heart-Tokushima.

"I just got off the phone with American Airlines. They told me they would not fly animals today anyway. It's too cold! It must be 7-8 degrees Celsius (about 45 Fahrenheit)! He told me to try FedEx."

Update

I have confirmation that both Japanese Earthquake Animal Rescue and Support along with WorldVets have reached out to her and are hoping that they can reach a solution that will allow for peace of mind when she leaves with her children on Friday (Japanese time). The situation at this point is that *no* airline will fly animals out of the country from her location due to the weather, which is very cold and in some places it is even snowing, hampering rescue and relief efforts for sure but at the same time making it unsafe and against airline policy to fly animals. The temperature outside must be above a certain cutoff point in order for animals to fly cargo; this is for their health. The family's desperate situation and forced departure is overwhelming. My last communication from her was that she is desperate to find an airline that will fly the two dogs and two cats when she leaves and not have to leave them behind, even if there are promises to get the animals to her and that they will be cared for in the interim.

I feel like the only way to get them out at this point is via private plane or transport that would allow the dogs and cats to be in the cabin (crated) so they can be in the temperature-regulated area with the family. I don't know that either the private plane or transport will be found in time to help this family.

There are likely other families begin forced to make the same decision: leave because the military is evacuating them. Because it is an evacuation and not a change of orders, they are being forced to leave their pets behind. If the base is evacuating there will be no one left (or possibly only a very minimal support staff) who will be able to watch the animals until other arrangements are made. It's not like they can ask their neighbors or friends to keep them for a week or two until things have calmed down—no one will be left. Please continue to keep in mind this particular family and all the families being evacuated and forced to leave their pets behind, whether they are with the military or with private companies.

As more information becomes available, I will update. I have messaged the family but wanted to post to give anyone still awake tonight the ability to reach out to their contacts.

If you can help transport the two dogs and two cats along with the family, please contact me, and I will put you in touch with the family.

Update on Military Family Evacuation for their Pets
March 17, 2011

Before I share Mariaelena's post with all of you, I personally wanted to thank you for helping, for spreading this family's story, and for trying to get them home together. Thank you for every single tweet and Facebook share, telephone call and face to face telling of this family's story. This was truly a global community effort and you all shined.

I have seen the power of pet bloggers in action before, but this was the first truly global effort I have been involved with. It was your love and passion for animals that alerted WorldVets and Japan Earthquake Animal Rescue and Support (JEARS) to this family's plight and had them responding and corresponding with the family within hours of the plea hitting the Internet. WorldVets offered to transport the two dogs and two cats with one of their team members who needed to get back to the U.S. in the coming days. JEARS opened their shelter and said they would hold the dogs and cats as long as it would take for arrangements to be made in order to get them home; all that would need to be done was to figure out a way to drive the animals to the shelter location.

Within 12 hours, Pets for Patriots had contacted me with information to try and help the family. I was also contacted by a reporter for *Stars and Stripes*, the U.S. military newspaper, to try and find out more details of the situation. I have received emails, private messages and tweets from people all over the world trying to offer suggestions for the family as well as their love and support.

From Mariaelena:

"I need to say a HUGE thank you to everyone who responded. I got a lot of good information, emails, phone calls and advice. Unfortunately, I will not be able to fly my pets back to California by Friday with us. I did get many calls and emails about plenty of local rescues here in Japan. My husband is due home shortly, and I will have a neighbor check in on them.

My husband will take care of evacuating them, along with assisting the rest of the base when the time comes. I can only imagine how many other people there are in my situation. I've shared all information that I got here with the community. Susie has been a HUGE help. I don't know how I can ever repay her. She truly has a heart of gold. It will be good to be somewhere safe, but I have a heavy heart about leaving my beloved pets behind.

I have to have faith in the people who know what they are talking about and hope that my husband and the animals can get out safely if and when they need to. I never imagined having to be separated from my husband during a time like this. But I trust him. I'll update everyone, including the personal emails and FB posts I got as soon as I land.

Thank you from the bottom of my heart." -Mariaelena ♥

Another Update from the Military: Family Pets Are Safe for Now
March 20, 2011

I know that many of you are still concerned for the pets of military families in Japan. As long as I keep receiving updates, I will continue to publish them for all of you. Mariaelena is now home in the U.S., safe with her children but concerned for her husband and pets back in Japan. The situation in the devastated areas of Japan is still horrible, however, as more and more organizations are able to make their way into these areas, people will be able to feel more hope for the future. WorldVets and JEARS plan to be in the worst hit areas by Tuesday to offer help to as many animals as possible.

Latest update from Mariaelena:

"I just got an update from my husband, who arrived home in Japan just after I left. He is home with the animals and back to work to help with the evacuation efforts. At this time, all evacuations are voluntary. Thankfully, they are accepting pets on flights now! I'm so happy something was finally done about this issue. Unfortunately, I'm already gone. But, I have put my trust in my husband to take them with him IF and WHEN he must evacuate. Most of my worries about their being left alone are put at ease; I just wish they could have made it home with me. I'd love a reason to go for a walk with my dogs or to curl up on the couch with my kitties.

I can only hope and pray that everything goes well in the Tsunami stricken areas, that pets get reunited with their owners and the ones that can't get good forever homes. I'm willing to help in any way I can from California, and of course, when I return to Japan. Thank you for all you do."

http://woofreport.com/

Woof Report

Woof Report.com is a website and free weekly email newsletter for dog lovers featuring pup-perfect dog care and training tips, news, handpicked products, tips for helping animal welfare causes and more.

Favorite Posts:

Fifteen Tips to Make 2011 a Fantastic Year for Your Dog
January 05, 2011

If you've already made your New Year's resolutions, it's time to turn to the well-being of your dog. It's a new year and the perfect opportunity to establish new routines that will make 2011 your dog's healthiest and happiest year yet. Here are some ideas to get you started.

Prepare for the Unexpected. Add the numbers of a 24/7 animal poison control center and your

Behind the Blog:
Stacey Sachs

Inspired By:
Larry (Border Collie/Lab mix) and Ted (tabby cat)

Kitty Condo:
California

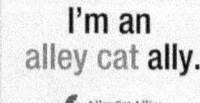

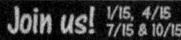

nearest 24/7 vet hospital to your cell phone, and place the numbers near your home phone. Create a pet first-aid kit, and place a pet rescue window alert on an outside window of your home to notify firefighters there are pets inside.

ID check. Make sure your dog's ID tags and microchip records are updated if your phone number or address has changed. And if your dog is not microchipped, visit your vet or seek a local clinic to get it done.

Exercise together. Walk your pup at least twice a day to burn off extra calories, release pent-up energy and keep your dog healthy. He or she will love you for it, and it's good for you, too! See Woof Report's new tip How to Get Fit with Your Dog's Help for tips on exercising with your dog.

Let the games begin. Engage your dog in mental exercise as well with treat dispensing and puzzle toys and a weekly game of hide-and-seek. And vow to teach your dog of any age (older dogs included) a new trick every other week or once a month. Download 101 Tricks to Teach Your Dog from the Dog Scouts for ideas, and then Google the name of the trick to find instructions, or pick up Kyra Sundance's fun instructional book, *101 Dog Tricks*.

Visit the vet. Schedule a vet visit to make sure your dog is in good health. Keep your pup up-to-date on vaccinations and maintain a regular schedule of heartworm and flea and tick preventives. These items are essential for your dog's good health.

Create a dog health record. Stop by WoofReport.com to download a free Dog Health History form. It's all you need to track your dog's health and help your dog's vet provide better care.

Feed your dog well. Take time to research your dog's food and the other options that are available to make sure he's getting the very best. Visit the independent websites dogfoodproject.com or dogfoodadvisor.com to see how various brands stack up.

Groom on. Commit to maintaining a good grooming schedule. Regular brushing, bathing, nail clipping and weekly teeth brushing all keep your dog healthy, comfortable and looking good.

Try something new. Take a class with your dog—anything from a refresher course with a trainer to maintain your dog's good behavior to fun classes like agility and flyball offered at your local SPCA. Or maybe this is your dog's year to help others and look into training him to become a therapy dog!

Help a shelter. Not all pets are as lucky as yours, so help pets in need by donating money, goods or your time (your dog will be happy to share you for a good cause). There are many ways to volunteer – from taking photos of shelter pets, to fostering and posting profiles of available pets online. Begin with a minimal time commitment if it makes it easier to get started.

Start a pet savings account. Regularly put aside money in a dedicated savings account or simply in tuck it an envelope and use it for vet care, grooming or even a new collar when your dog's wardrobe needs a boost.

Research resources. This is your year to lock in good pet-sitting resources long before you schedule a trip. Take the time now to read reviews, visit facilities and meet pet sitters to find just the right fit for dog care while you're away.

Spend quality time with your dog. Give your dog your undivided attention each and every day. Play with your dog or cuddle on the couch and give your pup an extended ear rub. And get to know and understand your dog's likes and dislikes to improve and strengthen your bond.

Clean the pup stuff. Round up all of your dog's toys and give them a good washing (see Woof Report's past tip on cleaning your dog's toys), and launder all your dog's bedding. Then make a plan to keep up the clean – for instance, wash your dog's toys the first of each month and your dog's bedding every other time you wash your sheets.

Read the Woof Report. Keep reading Woof Report to learn how to best care for your dog, and sign up for Woof Report Weekly Email newsletters so you don't miss a tip! Please share *Woof* with others with dogs too.

All about Paw Preference in Dogs
March 16, 2011

Are dogs left-pawed or right-pawed, or do they show any paw preference at all? And does it mean anything if they show a preference for using one paw over another?

Interestingly enough, dogs and many other animals are are right- or left-pawed, and many are also ambidextrous. While numerous studies have been conducted looking for gender and breed differences in terms of 'pawedness' in dogs, most studies show varying results, although many show male dogs having a left paw preference. On a related note, a 2009 study from the School of Psychology, Queen's University Belfast found that female cats showed a greater preference for using their right paws while males were more inclined to use their left paws. (Read more about the study on cats at the link below.)

How do you determine your dog's paw preference?

If you are right handed, you may perceive your dog to be left-handed since he or she mirrors your actions – for instance, when you ask for a paw to shake. Below are a number of ways paw preference is commonly determined. Use one or more of these methods to test your pup and repeat the tests to look for patterns.

- Place a treat under the couch and just within reach of your dog to see which paw she uses to reach for it.
- Watch which paw your dog uses to hold a bone with while chewing on it.
- Place a piece of adhesive tape on your dog's snout (just for a minute!) to look at which paw she uses to remove it.

- Watch which paw your dog uses first in stepping forward.

And the method used in many research studies, place a treat-filled Kong directly in front of your dog to see which paw he uses to hold it to get the food out. A dog may use either paw or both paws.

Does paw preference affect behavior?

Research studies being conducted now and in the past have connected paw preference with certain behaviors and temperaments. For instance, a 2006 University of New England study from Dr. Nick Branson found the way dogs use their paws may be a sign of how they react to noise. More specifically, findings revealed ambidextrous dogs (those without a paw preference) are likely to be more reactive to noise such as thunderstorms and fireworks.

According to Branson, "It seems possible that dogs that do not favour one side or the other may be prone to experience intense emotional responses to a broad range of stimuli. Animals with lateralised functions may be able to transfer attention from disturbing stimulus more successfully."

Branson adds this research may help save time and money in training working dogs for sniffing and bomb detection work since fear of noise is a common reason why dogs are rejected from such programs. Trainers will be able to select the most suitable dogs for specific jobs using paw preference as an indicator.

According to Dr. Paul McGreevy, an animal behavior expert at University of Sydney's Faculty of Veterinary Science and another expert on the topic, the use of such predictors can also save time and money when it comes to training guide dogs. With only about half of guide dogs passing training programs successfully, resources can be allocated to dogs with the highest probability for success.

For more on this interesting topic, explore the links below. And don't forget to put your dog through the simple tests to determine his or her paw preference!

The scoop:

Read the interview with Dr. Paul McGreevy, "How much of a successful working dog's behaviour is linked to being left or right pawed?" http://www.abc.net.au/ra/innovations/stories/s1772249.htm

Read about Dr. Nick Branson's research, "How does handedness affect behaviour?" http://www.ozpets.com.au/articles/400/dogbehaviour.html/

Read about paw preference in cats, "Female Cats Are Right-Pawed, Males Are Lefties" http://dsc.discovery.com/news/2009/07/23/cats-handedness

The Top 12 iPhone Apps for Dog Care, Play and More
February 09, 2011

Now that the much-anticipated Verizon iPhone is here, it's just the time to take another look at some of the practical and fun iPhone apps created for dog owners. When Woof Report last featured some of Apple's apps for the iPhone and iPod Touch, the app store offered 30,000 apps of all kinds, which sounded like a lot — and now there are more than 300,000!

Below are some of the best apps for dog owners. Download them to your iPhone, iPod Touch or iPad to find dog-friendly locales, off-leash parks, pet first aid tips, and more; many are free or cost just $.99 each. And if your favorites are missing from the list, please add them to the *Comments* section on the site.

Dog Park Finder

Near home or on the go, the Dog Park Finder app powered byDogParkUSA. com has you covered with listings of 2,400+ dog parks. Using your phone's GPS, it finds the nearest park, and includes photos, user reviews and details, such as if it's fenced, has small dog areas and the hours and days of operation. FREE.

Paw Card

With the Paw Card app, create an unlimited number of profiles for your dogs, cats, and other pets to keep track of their vital information and always have it with you. Record your pet's ID tag numbers and vet contacts, and track your pet's medications, medical and vaccination history, and more. That's not all. Email your pet's Paw Card to your dog walker, pet sitter, or vet. FREE.

Petfinder

Search pets by breed, age, gender and size from 13,000 shelters and rescue groups around the country with the Petfinder app. It's just what you need when someone tells you they'd like to *buy* a pet, or if you're looking for a new family member. Bookmark your favorite pet profiles and share them with friends via email, Facebook and Twitter. FREE.

Pet First Aid

Be prepared with the Pet First Aid app and you'll have instant access to clear, concise advice for common pet emergencies. With detailed articles, video and illustrations, you'll know exactly how to care for your pet. Learn how to handle bites and stings, bandaging, burns, bleeding, fractures, poisoning and much more. $3.99.

FidoFactor

Locate all the dog-friendly spots in your area with the FidoFactor app - dog parks, dog friendly restaurants, bars, pet stores, hotels and more. And not only will you find directions, hours and contact information in its growing user-generated database, but you'll find user reviews, too. FREE.

MixItUp with Adopt-a-Pet.com

Take a gamble on the MixItUp with Adopt-a-Pet.com app that allows you to seamlessly insert your dog (or cat, or your significant other) into three famous paintings from the classic 1903 Brown & Bigelow "Dogs Playing Poker" calendar. The best part, a percentage of the proceeds from each download is donated to Adopt-a-Pet.com. $.99.

Pet Acoustics

With the Pet Acoustics app, you'll get music specifically designed for the hearing sensitivities of your pet in terms of frequency, volume and rhythm. Use it to calm and soothe your pet for rest time, car travel, veterinary visits and at other times. $1.99.

Best of 101 Dog Tricks

Teach your old or young dog a few new tricks with the Best of 101 Dog Tricks app. The app includes eight tricks from Kyra Sundance's best-selling book, *101 Dog Tricks*, and teaching your dog the tricks is a snap with video, photos and step-by-step instructions. $.99.

iKnowDogs

Download the iKnowDogs app and become an absolute expert on dog breeds. This detailed reference guide includes over 1,200 photos and facts about AKC-recognized dog breeds, and lets you identify dogs by appearance, temperament, purpose and country of origin. $3.99.

iSqueek

Always have a squeaky toy on hand to get your dog's attention, thanks to the iSqueek app, a virtual squeak-toy that reacts realistically to your touch. Press on any of the 18 toys, each with its own sound, to create long or short sound bursts to which your dog will respond. (Have plenty of praise or a treat for your dog to make up for the fact he doesn't actually receive a squeaky toy when he responds!) $1.99.

Pet Services Finder

Find all the services for your pet's needs at home or on the road. The Pet Services Finder helps you locate the nearest veterinarians, emergency clinics, doggie daycare facilities, dog sitters and walkers, dog groomers and more. Once the results appear, it's your choice: click to call, get directions or read and post reviews. FREE.

PetSnap

Pictures of your dog on your phone are a must, and the PetSnap app improves your odds of taking a great shot. The app offers 32 different sounds to instantly get your dog's attention, perfect for getting him or her to look right into the camera. $1.99.

The scoop:

Those with cats, be sure to download the CatPaint app, which lets you effortlessly add all or any of sixteen adorable cats to your photos.

All about a Dog's Sense of Taste
February 23, 2011

With dogs, it's all about the power of the nose.

Stories detailing the amazing capabilities of a dog's sense of smell continually appear in the news. Detection of various cancers? Check. Detection of bombs and explosives? Check. Detection of toxic mold and bed bugs? Check. Detection of wildlife 'scat' to aid wildlife conservation? Check. Detection of a can of cat food being opened while napping? Check!

But how about a dog's sense of taste? Given the unusual and downright unappetizing things you've probably seen your dog eat (doggie 'business' and grass sandwiches, anyone?), you probably already know a dog's sense of taste is not well developed. And it comes as no surprise. After all, a dog's sense of smell is extraordinary, and a dog's sense of hearing is excellent, so it would seem unusual that all of the senses of one particular species would be so highly developed.

Read on for interesting facts about your best friend's sense of taste.

Dogs have about 1,700 taste buds in their mouths, while humans have about 9,000, and our feline friends only around 470.

Although a dog's sense of taste is the least developed of his or her senses, dogs are capable of detecting bitter, sweet, salty and sour tastes. Humans and cats detect the same four, although it was previously believed cats could not taste sweets. In humans, a fifth taste called *umami* or 'savory' was recently recognized in the West as a basic taste, and a 1991 research study determined that dogs showed taste responses to "umami substances."

A dog's sense of taste and smell are considered to be closely linked, with dogs likely gathering more information about the food they eat from its smell versus taste.

Most of a dog's taste buds are centered around the tip of the tongue.

Studies show a dog will avoid eating a particular food that has caused sickness in the past for a certain amount of time; it's an instinctive protective mechanism.

Along with touch, taste is the only sense developed in dogs at birth.

The most abundant taste buds in dogs are those that respond to sugars or sweet tastes.

http://happytailsbooks.com/blog

Bonus Blog: Happy Tails Books

Behind the Blog: Kyla Duffy

Inspired By: Bill (adopted Boston Terrier)

Doghouse: Colorado

We've come to the end of this edition of *15 Great Pet Blogs,* but it's only fair that we get to share a favorite post from our own blog, too. Right?

Inspired by Bill, a rescued puppy mill survivor, the Happy Tails Books blog mainly covers Kyla Duffy's experiences as a foster parent for MidAmerica Boston Terrier Rescue, spotlights on rescue organizations around the country, occasional product reviews and, of course, some "happy tails" about adopted pets.

Favorite Posts:

Mill Mommas and Mistletoe
November 16, 2010

Everywhere you turn during the months approaching Christmas, you see signs saying things like, "Christmas is a time for giving."

Because this giving is regulated to happen every 12 months, it can easily become automatic, lacking profound thought.

For me the holidays even began to feel like a chore – too much to do, not enough money, too little time. I always looked forward to our family holiday parties, where video game bowling tournaments have become a tradition alongside the eggnog and spiced rum, but other than that the holidays often seemed more like a time for stress than a time for cheer.

Several years ago we became a foster family for MidAmerica Boston Terrier Rescue. We didn't know anything about puppy mills at the time, but we got a crash course via our first few foster dogs. Each one was unique, but none was quite like Zoye, our 20th foster dog who came to us just before last Christmas. She had been a breeding dog at a mill, stuck in a chicken wire cage 24/7, perpetually making puppies for SEVEN years. Her splayed paws and droopy nipples said it all. Our rescue had adopted her out to a "good" home, but after six months I was asked if I would pick her up and take her in as a foster. Odd, I thought, and just before the holidays?

Zoye, a 7 ½-year-old mill momma who doesn't let anything stop her

I met Zoye's "mom" in a hotel parking lot, where she handed me a dog in a too-small crate. She said Zoye had "bitten both dogs and children, could not be potty trained, and must be deaf and blind because she keeps walking into things." She had locked Zoye in her kitchen for six months where Zoye's urine couldn't damage the floor. I'm glad she didn't invite me over to eat!

On the drive home, I worried. Caring for an incontinent, blind biter over the holidays in addition to my two cats and Bill, a quirky puppy mill survivor we had adopted, was not going to be easy. I imagined Zoye's first introduction to my house: a trail of pee following her like breadcrumbs and a vicious battle with Bill, leaving him ear-less. It seemed my Christmas was going to be spent scrubbing floors and breaking up fights.

What occurred, in reality, was… Merry! Zoye made friends with Bill immediately and then claimed a squeaky toy for her own, proudly parading it around the house. She did have accidents, but it was clear she could be trained. Where was the deaf, blind devil dog? Why wasn't she walking into walls?

Zoye and Bill at the family Christmas Party

That Christmas our holiday party had a new star – Zoye! She marched around my parents' house – the whole house, not just the kitchen – as if everyone had come just to greet her. She sported a little diaper like a fashion accessory and snuggled on the couch with Bill to watch our highly-competitive (only to my dad, mind you) bowling tournament. The pair was the picture of contentment in each other's warmth.

You may not have known it, but I accepted it for us all, and on behalf of all the dogs adopted out of mills who leave their pasts behind. It's the gift that Zoye gave me, and you, and the miller, and the woman who locked her in the kitchen. She gave us *all* the gift of forgiveness by licking and loving and living without a shadow of resentment or regret. The gift was a lesson, one for which I remain grateful and steadfast in my service as a foster home and advocate for Zoye and dogs like her. Maybe those signs should say, "Christmas is a time 'forgiving,' " instead.

This year's mistletoe mill momma: Olive

This year the holidays seem right – a time for cheer. If Zoye could leave her stress behind her, so can I. Plus, Zoye is in a truly loving home now, and we'll be spending this holiday with our new mill momma foster dog, Olive. No diaper needed… as of last week.

Editors' note: It's funny how things come full circle. The editors didn't plan it this way, but it turns out Yvonne DiVita from BlogPaws is connected to both the introduction and conclusion of this book. Not only did Yvonne write the beautiful introduction, but she also adopted Olive earlier this year, the dog in the above photo! Yvonne knows both blogs and rescue, and we salute her for her diligent efforts to make this world a friendlier, safer place for our pets.

A Final Word

We hope you enjoyed the blog posts included in this book. Your learning and enjoyment doesn't have to end here! As you surely have noticed, each chapter header includes information on how you can access more posts from your favorite authors online. They'll greatly appreciate it if you pay them a visit, read their blog and share your feedback through the comments section at the end of each post. Most of the bloggers can also be found on Twitter and Facebook by searching for the author's name or blog title.

About Happy Tails Books™

Happy Tails Books™ sells books and gifts that raise awareness and funding for animal rescue organizations. Their flagship *Lost Souls: Found!* series features stories from people who have fostered and adopted animals. These books serve not only to entertain but also to educate readers about dog adoption and the characteristics of different breeds. Happy Tails Books™ donates a significant portion of proceeds back to the rescue groups that help gather stories for the books.

To submit a story or learn about other books Happy Tails Books™ publishes, please visit our website at http://happytailsbooks.com.

www.ingramcontent.com/pod-product-compliance
Lightning Source LLC
Chambersburg PA
CBHW071707040426
42446CB00011B/1957